Eutopian Dreams

Expressing Good Places

Eutopian Dreams
Expressioning Good Places

A. M. Caratheodory

Calliope Press
Sarasota
2008

The author thanks: Violet Reason for the reuse of some of her
phrases from *Cheap Visions* and *Retreads*. Alan Wittbecker, for
relating his ideas from *Eutopias* in the Introduction. The editors and
publishers, especially on internet sites, who criticized or published
many of these works earlier.   (AM@Caratheodory.info)

The following poems have been published previously:
Amaryllis (1977), *Sawtooth*; The Ground (1976), *Luckiamute IV*;
Walking (1980), *Honey Creek Anthology*; Amphibian Dreams (1980),
Wellspring; Leaves (1967), *Blue Hen Review*; Fossils (1982), *FourMile
Creek Review;* Three Nights in the Heart of the Earth (1983),
Windrow; Paradox of Metal, *Emerald* (1976), Touching, *Emerald*
(1976); From Umbriel Observed, *Transition* (1976); Cocoon of
Light, Transition (1976); Perception like Candlelight, *Fourmile
Creek Review* (1978); Modern Geology, *Palouse Hills* (1980);
Clothes of Silence Laid Aside, *Palouse Hills (1980);* Leaving
Palouse, *Daily News (Moscow)* (1998).

Graphics by Rian Garcia Calusa, Tallevast, Florida
    (Design@riangarciacalusa.com)

Library of Congress Cataloging-in-Publication data
Alain M. Caratheodory, 1946—
Light from a vanished forest/A. M. Caratheodory

I. Title.
PS3553.A644A801 2008
ISBN 978-0-911385-40-3 (paper)
Manufactured in the United States of America

First Printing
A Calliope Press Book, Mozart and Reason Wolf, Ltd.
    (Mozart@reasonwolf.com)

Contents

Introduction, by Alan Wittbecker

Weeds
Walter and Bessie
Winona Stars
Accomplishments
Past is Only a Tool
Did I not also
Remembering Decades
Nexus of Permanence
Darkness Still
Lightbearer

Sweet Flowers Bitter Fruits   Other Lovers
Place of reconciliation
Dancing in the Dark
Two Galaxies
Eidolon Lost
What it was was
Her Plea / First Dream
Aurum Nostrum
That's all / Memento Mori
Why You're bad for Me
Wing of Your Eye

Microscopia   Bridge of Light
Wild Apples   Amaryllis
Bastet
Counting Universes
The Ground
Origin of Myth
Clothes of Silence Laid Aside
Perception like Candlelight
Wild Apples
Aphrodite's Fruit
Cocoon of Light
Dream of Dionysius
From Umbriel Observed
With Locust Flowers
October Light
Ille Terrarum

	Failing Sleep
	Just a Smile
	Leaving Palouse
	Knowing Why
	Altazor Forest Passage
Fragments	Aeakus Humbled
	Tantalus
	Antaeus & Herakles
	Odysseus
	Penelope
	Children of Ankaa
	Heraklitus' Dream
	Phoenix
	Shadow of the Mistress of the World
	The Others
	Daphne
	Authentic Fragments of Leukippus
Ancient Light	Small Dark Windows
	Dark Moon
	Binary
	Observing Mountain Light
	Black Sun Waiting
	Contemplating Speech
Amphibian Dreams	Lilith
	Three Nights in the Heart of the Earth
	Alone in a World of Wounds
	Metaphysics of Order
	Signs
	Sea Anemone & Crab
	Way of the Deer
	Wolf
	Wolf News
	Shadow Play
	Wolf Loves to Hide
	Convolutions
	Bear Masks
	Cave of Night
Forest Light	Weeds
	Lives of Weeds
	Ecstasy of Weeds

Hamadryad Hiding
Amphibian Dreams
Night in an Irish Forest
Three perspectives from an Irish Forest
    September
    February
    November
    April
    June
Haiku Interlude
False Senryu Word Nests
Paion

Facets of Light   Riashamimi Reflected
Miriamisha in Tearlight
Amamishari in Dreams
Shamirimia in Silk
Mariamishi in Wild Flight
Horses Under Lightning
Wild Strawberries
Marishimia Dancing
Evening Swifts
Gathering Layers
Threads
Changing Light
Leaf

Masks   Moon as Mask for the Earth
Dust as Mask for Chaos
Metal as Mask for Energy
The Visible as Mask for the Invisible
Sound as Mask for the Visible
Light as Mask for the Dark
Shadow as Mask for Light
Flesh as Mask for Shadow
Consciousness as Mask for Flesh
Sleep as Mask for Consciousness
Dreams as Mask for Sleep

About the Author
Colophon

Dedication

Dedicated to *Marishimia* (Precious Woulfe)—who displays so many facets when she is reflecting light, and not absorbing it or slowing it.

Quidquid sub terra est, in apricum proferet aetas;
Defodiet condetque nitentia.   Horace

(Time will bring to light whatever is hidden;
it will cover up and conceal what is now shining in splendor.)

A western redcedar wildlife tree at Altazor Forest

Making Good Places with Good Dreams and Good Work
Alan Wittbecker

This book is a series of poetic expressions of good places. Like
the author, my friend and neighbor at Altazor Forest, I lived in
Northern Idaho, just upstream. I am familiar with many of the
places he is writing about. Like the author, I am familiar with the
history of utopian thought and its influence on communities and
places. I want to introduce those thoughts that, along with ecology
and dream-states, have influenced his poetry.

No Place Sounds Like Good Place

The City, Amanote, speaks to introduce herself in Thomas
More's 1516 fantasy, *Utopia*, about a perfect commonwealth, a
society without the problems and poverty of an immature English
capitalism. While relating his story in Latin, More made puns on
the Greek names he used: The name of the city, Amanote, means
"dream town." The name of the traveler himself, Hythlodae,
means "dispenser of nonsense." The title is also a word play, a pun;
to the Greek word meaning place (*topia*), could be added a prefix
meaning no (*ou*), or good (*eu*). More removed the first letter and
used 'u' as an ambiguous prefix—no place sounded like good place.
The citizens in More's utopia were uniform and regimented:
Everyone had the same clothing, housing, and work schedule.
Strong peer pressure existed for people to use their leisure time
constructively for the public good or to improve their personal
virtues. The electoral unit, the family, was autocratically ruled by
the patriarch and a hierarchy of princes. Decisions were made by
councils elected from public officials, who met regularly with these
princes.

Only a few hours of labor a day for everyone would be
sufficient to supply all the necessities and comforts of life. The
residents of Utopia rejected beautiful clothing, although we
now understand much more about the importance of aesthetic
needs. Having everyone have one simple garment would not
be acceptable now. People like to improve things. Clothing, for
instance, can reflect differences in taste or status, and people will
devote much time and money to clothing. In Utopia, money is
eliminated, and therefore many crimes no longer exist, although
we understand much more about the human need for prestige and

9

honor. People do kill and cheat for prestige and honor as often as for any gold or symbols. For More, Nature deserves respect, if for no other reason than she is capable of turning against us, and must be treated with care, although he also regarded nature as endless, to be converted to cities and fields with each new utopian colony. And, we now understand that large tracts of wilderness are necessary to provide supporting services to human enclaves.

Utopias are fictions by definition. More had said that it was a fiction whereby the truth might "slide into men's minds." More's utopia is meant to be a description of an achieved egalitarian society. More expected that part of the meaning of Utopia would be carried in the dialogues inspired by the book. Chronologically, More created a good place first, and a society constructed from his own moral and rational ideals second. As More wrote, he realized that humans can make any good place less good, that they can seek less than the optimum, or reinvent original sin. Human nature creates conditions that reverse its good. Absurdities are invented, toyed with, and embraced. It is human nature, to attempt to escape all control, or to express the desire to be wicked. More's vision had an immediate effect on literature and ideas, but less of an effect on the growth and development of his country.

Utopian thought can be found in almost every culture, in prophecies, visions, dreams, myths, and ideologies. In general, utopias have been preoccupied with static societies that were egalitarian and open. They tended to emphasize a purposive world characterized by a moral order. They usually tended to refer to the past or future, and to theocratic salvation or rational achievement. Utopias are not just visions of nowhere, but of otherness.

Other images of the world, different from the unplanned, unconscious, political realisms, are dismissed as being unrealistic. Utopias have been offered as ideal schemes for social and political development. But, such utopias tend to require too much change, rejecting the past or refusing the cultural present, then creating new institutions out of nothing. Utopias are often rejected as irrelevant dreams and self-indulgent imaginings. Yet, as Pierre Dansereau has said, the failures of pollution, poverty, and urban decay are failures of imagination. Rejecting the solutions of imagination, therefore, can only make the modern suite of crises worse. Dreams and imagination are needed to describe desirable futures, to support plans, and to outline goals.

Poetry of Dreams and Mythology

The first function of a living mythology, the religious function according to Joseph Campbell, is to waken and maintain in an individual the experience of awe and respect in recognition of the ultimate mystery that transcends words and names—from which words turn back (the word mythos originally meant 'mute'). Myths are ways of teaching unobservable realities by way of observable symbols. This is so the individual has an identity. The second function of mythology is to provide a cosmology, an image of the universe. In fact, the world has to be recognized and assimilated by the mythopoetic imagination. Myth weaves human knowledge, skills and aspirations together in intersubjective realm of image that blends science and art. Mythic symbols can store and convey vast amounts of information concisely. Myth describes the range of behavior that ordinary people are capable of. Myths teach what it is important to know to live in a place. The third mythological function is the validation and maintenance of an established order.

Mythology can join science with feeling to help us change to adapt to our surroundings. Mythology is not limited by method. Mythic symbols store information concisely, which makes it possible for a person to assimilate the collective experiences of a culture. Myth combines us with other beings. Mythologies are in fact great poems that function to awaken the experience of awe and humility that one feels before a mystery. They also bring the individual into harmony with the whole. High human cultures must depend on renewable resources, from photosynthesis to wind, tide, and sun, to continue "making" good places for people in a culture.

Poetry is literally a form of making. To 'make' means 'to bring into being' or produce something physically or mentally (from the English and Germans words, from the Greek word meaning to 'knead,' press and stretch dough). Poetry also means to build, fit, or create. The making of a home would be an 'ecopoetic' activity (from the Greek word fragments for 'house-making').

Poetry is communicative of the quality of things. Like science, it discriminates the unsuspected in the commonplace. It is not different from science, but more diffuse. It is not better than science, but more comprehensive. It accepts ontological parity, the equality of beings; aspects of the world are not negated or reduced by one another. As metaphorical knowledge, which

11

may be prerational or metarational, poetry can avail itself of scientific references. Poetry can measure a whole qualitatively and mimetically, a germ or the cosmos with its imagery. Poetry is a tool for comprehending partially what cannot be known totally. A poetic language could include a view of the interrelatedness of all existence in a sublime ecology.

People need to be made aware of the power of self-determination. People need to feel things, like the immensity and uniqueness of nature or the strangeness of a biting tick, before they can act. Poetry can help people feel themselves as part of the web of life or on an oasis in space. That feeling, more than any laws or injunctions, can justify preserving the ecological systems of the earth on which we live. That is one thing Caratheodory does: Try to express the immensity or strangeness of nature. Humanity is a poetic species, as Richard Rorty noted, "one which can change its behavior by the words it uses." We need desperately to change our behavior, from our thoughtless interference and destruction of natural patterns, to a fitness with them.

Poetry expresses the image of human potential, of what other circumstances may have formed. Poetry tells of a goal, even if it is the moral superiority of suffering in the 'third world.' By presenting a goal, poets can become the "unacknowledged legislators of mankind," as Percy Bysshe Shelley defined them. Poetry creates a fourth world, of groups sharing part of the wealth of the earth in a global community. This fourth world is where the past is reconciled with the present and the terrible beauty of the future is born. The terror of beauty, as Rainer Maria Rilke recognized, results from its power to shake humans from the refuge of a small identity into an immense strange world surrounding them.

The lives of humans and all beings has become a collective responsibility. Humanity has to learn to live on a finite and varied earth. Learning is a transforming experience, but difficult. Poetry objectifies conscious experience and makes it easier to communicate. Poetry shows the diversity of human experience. Poetry gives groups and individuals their identity; it articulates societies and authenticates forms of exchange. By transcending the limits of single cultures, it draws all cultures together. The tradition of poetry does not belong to just three human worlds; it encompasses them and links them together in a fourth.

The Ecology of Place

The use of the word "ecology" by Ernst Haeckel implied that the natural world was a place to live, a house, rather than a machine to control. Making the earth into a house is fundamentally a poetic activity, according to Gaston Bachelard. Poetry is a way of understanding the universe through metaphor, a literary device that transfers the characteristics of one term to another. As Picasso said of art, poetry also is a 'lie that tells the truth.' For example, William Shakespeare said "The body is a garden" and William Harvey said "the body is a machine." The body is not a garden or a machine, but the metaphors extend our understanding of the body.

If poetry is a way of expressing myths and dreams, then the science of ecology, studied through its components and relations, is a perspective, a way of "seeing," according to Paul Shepard. It is a perspective of the human situation in its interconnection. For Paul Sears, ecology is a "subversive subject." Ecology is nonreductive, integrative, and amphibious, having the authority of science and the force of morals. It is normative and sensible. Ecology also offers a "sacramental vision" of nature. Ecology is radical—from the Latin word meaning "rooted"—and forms part of a new metaphor that is more appropriate to the unity and interrelatedness of the earth. Caratheodory uses the perspective of ecology to describe connections between the moon and the earth, or between the bluebird and its housebuilder. Ecology is part of a movement of consciousness, concerned with equality, diversity, health, with humane methods, and with a holopoetic cosmology, and ecology affects them simultaneously. Ecology offers a new perspective of humanity in the total field of nature and defines balanced relationships with ultrahuman beings and species. It urges local, self-reliant cultures with adaptive cosmologies and natural values in productive ecosystems. And, it can provide clues to making good places in wild ecosystems.

Making Good Places

The second meaning of utopia, 'eutopia,' is not used often. It means simply 'good place.' Good places do exist. They can be described, and even expanded. Some of the traits that make them good can be understood and repeated. A formal description of the general characteristics of good places, eutopias, can extend

13

utopian thought into ecology, as well as into anthropology and psychology. Perhaps the number of good places can be increased with understanding of traditional ways and with more effective metaphors. Good places, and good societies, can be partly understood through certain paths of ecology, economics and politics. Good places are often made by living in place for decades. Caratheodory understands this and expresses it succinctly.

Eutopian designs are more radical—in the sense of being rooted in reality. The word "utopian" was meant to be ambiguous. In a eutopian approach, that tries to be unambiguously good, utopian designs are replaced by realistic and achievable ones, that are based on new images of the earth and humanity. The eutopian plan tries to change human thinking, to use an ecological perspective, to ease human societies into partnership models, to restore wilderness and common places we have destroyed, and to change international relationships into a poetic framework capable of limiting war and permitting unique human expansion of cultural expressions. This approach suggests a global governing body to allow cultural independence. It outlines how to create places consciously, using our knowledge of how things work, but being aware of our ignorance, and by being careful and respectful. Certainly this seems more radical than continuing to surround ourselves with nuclear weapons and habitat destruction in the name of a political reality.

Unlike either the political realism of nations or the ideal designs of utopias, a eutopian approach relies on traditional human and cultural realities and proposes only modest and reasonable changes at local and international levels. Eutopias is way for preserving what is good and useful in human cultures and sciences, and for reserving what is necessary for nature to keep regenerating itself, while addressing the cascading problems of the modern expansion and catastrophic development with an emergency approach. Eutopias is a practical framework for allowing the creative anarchy of traditional-size cultures to be able to implement appropriate technology to deal with their resources and with other cultures through a revitalized and empowered international body that has the power of taxing global resources and properties for its own support, as well as the power to disarm and neutralize the unhealthy influences of large nations and corporations. Eutopias is a framework that limits human expansion to domestic and artificial areas, by specifying responsibilities and duties, while permitting the free operation of nature on the majority of the planet. It saves neopoetic areas and reserves wilderness. It encourages respect for natural and cultural capital. It recommends recognizing limits and planning for them using an ecological perspective and a metaphorical approach—it is metaphor-based as well as science-based, and limits-based as well as culture-based. Eutopias is concerned with saving human cultures and the environments that human cultures have come to fit in comfortably."

People exist in place. One secret to being successful and sustainable is to have the places be good places, so that people might develop their potentials. There are many potential levels of action, many ways of being, starting with the individual and continuing through the international. However, individuals are part of families, which are part of groups that often include extended families and regional communities.

From an ecological perspective, living organisms inter-penetrate deeply into nonliving forms and the earth. Individual organisms are woven into a complex fabric. Their activities reshape the fabric. Human beings, to make good places, have to consider their individual and social actions, their participation, as their responsibilities.

To make a good place, individual participation is necessary. Participation enters the constitution of place; it is not a fusion where things lose their identity, but a mutual infolding together where each becomes part of the identity of the other. Without it things would have no existence. To exist is to participate in place. Participations are felt, not thought. Participation leads to knowledge, science, and mystical experience.

Eutopias is a total reconsideration of the current pattern of technologies, cultures, value systems, and behaviors, evolving into a low-profile technological ethic suitable for a renaissance. It is a code for preserving those parts of the earth that are needed for renewing the holecosystem and for habitats for the billions of animals, plants and living beings that are part of the earth. It is a code for allowing fair use of that part of the earth that is human. It is a code for human equality in opportunity and worth. It is the demand for a margin from catastrophe, so that if humanity is unable to live peaceably, the rest of the earth will not become extinct as well.

The new theme for people's minds may begin in prose, but it should culminate in poetry. The human mind, under pressure from the dialectic process, grows into more subtle noetic experiences, until ecstatic insight blossoms. We must learn to be an individual in a human society in an ambihuman ecology with amphibian grace. To paraphrase a line from Keats, the poetry of the earth is never dead, but is could become unreadable to us, as remote as the stars. We must work out our direction through love; love is reverence for the experience of all beings. Through love, as well as through effort and intelligence, we humans can make good places on earth.

Doing Good Work
For 30 years, I lived on seventy acres south of Potlatch Idaho, northwest of Moscow mountain, on a small plateau with many north-facing draws. The flat had Ponderosa pines and Douglas firs surrounding a small meadow; the draws were filled with redcedar trees. The Altazor Forest is located in the No Name Creek watershed, which is part of the larger Flannagan Creek watershed, which is part of the Palouse River watershed, which drains into the Columbia Basin, and then into the Pacific Ocean.

The site had been logged heavily in the 1930s; much of the forest had been cleared for fields; virtually all of the rest of it had been cut using a variety of methods, from small clearcuts to sanitation cuts and individual tree selection. I found 5 slabwood piles and enough abandoned machinery to build an entire sawmill (later powered by a steam tractor).

I wanted to improve the health of the forest, so I created an ecological plan to continue using part of the forest, while restoring other parts. The primary concern of this kind of ecoforestry plan is to protect the framework of the forest for all forest organisms during human use. That means that the habitat of key species has to be preserved. Grandparent trees have to be protected in old-growth areas. Ecologically sensitive areas—steep or broken slopes, shallow soils, xeroscapes (really dry areas)—have to be used lightly, if at all. All riparian ecosystems (rivers, creeks, streams, lakes, ponds, wetlands—all water courses) should bear minimal human interference. Animal and plant corridors, especially cross-valley corridors that cross ridges between valleys, need to be maintained for critical movements; remember, many animals, such as bear and deer, require different habitat for eating, mating, and sleeping.

The result is an interconnected network of protected ecosystems extending throughout the forest.

Once the protected landscape network is established, the remaining forest areas are zoned for uses to provide for human and ambihuman needs. Forest use zones include culture, recreation-tourism, conservation, fish and wildlife, wilderness, trapping, timber, firewood, and alternative products. None of the uses in these zones should damage the forest.

Reforesting should be done when necessary. I used to have cows and horses in a pasture near the edge of the forest. I did not replace them after they died of old-age. Trees and shrubs were kept down by grazing, but recently have been invading the old pasture. The most heavily used part of the pasture is still shrubby, but other parts have been replanted, and natural regeneration has surpassed the planted areas in growth and diversity. The trees that were planted were planted in late winter; the seedlings were transplanted from skid roads and trails nearby. We do nothing for pest control other than cut down branches with dwarf mistletoe infestations.

At Altazor, there are only three skid roads and one haul road. There were more, but I have rehabilitated several skid trails, planted the haul road in wild grasses, and lined the banks with wild rose. Since the haul road cut across all three skid roads, no new roads have been built; the haul road crosses No-name Creek at 90 degrees across a culvert. The skid roads were built by hand and are only 3-4 feet wide—just about the tractor width; they are also planted. By contrast, when the neighbors to the south, at Twin Pine tree farm, had a salvage cut, a haul road was built on the east bank of the creek, causing tremendous erosion; their skid roads go straight up and down the hills, causing more erosion.

After an initial survey in 1976-77, with permanent quadrats and photo points, assessment has been more informal. Since I walk the woods every month, the community audits are less formal. I have two old growth areas (seed trees left consistently by loggers in the 1930s-60s), two natural nurseries, three aesthetic areas, and a 20-acre control stand, where no cutting is ever done.

For example, last week, I spent a day cutting (limbing and bucking) one fir tree. I also bucked a tree that had fallen across the power line to the pumphouse, started a fire for slash (from a pre-ownership 1961 cut), had a picnic lunch by the fire, walked around inspecting the general health of the forest, climbed a tree, played with the wolf, cleaned up the pumphouse, and walked home (1100 feet uphill).

People like to buy land with trees on it. Forests imply good business sense, individualism, healthy outdoor activities, including work, and adventure. Yes, adventure. Personally, the adventure extends from plants and animals to ideas. The Altazor Forest incorporates the territory of bears, mountain lions, coyotes, and others; for instance, one day I was gardening on the edge of the trees when a bear, 50-gallon barrel-size, ran along the garden, through the orchard and down the hill towards a spring—I was so surprised I just kept planting. I rarely see bears, but their evidence is everywhere in smashed logs, barked trees, and ravaged raspberries. Another time, I was walking along a trail reading and saw the neighbor's tan dog out of the corner of my eye standing in a clearing (our neighbors clearcut on the boundary to pay for a vacation to Canada). I reached out to pet him before I noticed the shape wasn't quite right—he was a male mountain lion just standing watching me. I stopped and looked at him; he looked, I looked; I looked, he flowed off down the hill. I started walking after him, until we were in deeper woods, then changed my mind after I lost sight of him, not wanting to be a nuisance or dinner. I see a lot of life in the forest. As I am writing this, two moose are loitering in the lower field (a pine nursery), having just come across from the western neighbor's cattle trails. At other times, I have raised orphan deer, bluebirds, crows, coyotes, garter snakes, and one skunk.

The forest teaches many things that we humans value. The forests teaches virtues, such as patience, frugality, and possibly self-reliance. The forest also teaches awareness of its limits and complexity. The forest is not something, like a computer game, that you can master in a day or even know completely in a decade or lifetime.

To integrate my gardens and orchard into the forest, I applied certain kinds of permaculture (after Bill Mollison), traditional farming with stands of trees (after Wendell Berry and others), natural farming where pines, cedars, and fruit trees are planted with grain and root crops (after Masanobu Fukuoka), and permanent tree crops, such as chestnut, honey locust, walnut, carob, grown on hills and mountains to complement flat-land agriculture (after J. Russell Smith). The common theme is the careful maintenance of the productivity of the land; industrial

18

tree farms, plantations, and orchards do not, in general, share this theme. Maintenance of productivity, or sustainability, has always been the goal of healthy cultures or agricultures.

Good Work in Good Places
Often, when working with other forest landowners, I am asked if I practice good forestry, and if I can apply it to the land in question. I usually describe the interactions of sowbugs and bluebirds, or canopy closure and root rot, to avoid a direct answer or a philosophical discussion of the meaning of the word "good." Philosophers have puzzled over the term "good" for centuries, constructing partial theories and contradictory systems. According to Plato, technical knowledge is not of ultimate importance for human beings because it knows nothing of "good itself." Knowledge of good is theoretical knowledge for him. The word "good" has an interesting and long history. The current version is derived from the old English, "god," meaning "suitable" or fitting, similar to the words meaning a "suitable time" and to be "suitable" or "pleasing." In an organic world, good things are defined by a free interplay of energies. Perhaps, as a working definition, we can just use "harmony." In Chinese medical tradition, the highest good is harmony, especially social harmony or good relations. A good person is one who creates and maintains harmony. Harmony is related to wholeness (indeed, the word "whole" comes from the Indo-European root "kailo," which is also the root for the words health and holy).

The use of the word "good" with forestry is problematic. Good means different things to different people. Your standards or codes, personally or culturally, might be different from mine. Therefore the meanings of the words will be different. The search for good is measured by personal criteria, personal judgment, and personal reflection. Furthermore, human beings cannot know, or even think of anything, according to Robert Zajonc, without some involvement of emotion, that is, at least a vague feeling of good or bad. On the other hand, there are questions of what one "ought" to do.

I still have trouble weighing good and bad in practice. I have no doubt that when I do more good, more bad is also created. For instance, when I started trying to restore Altazor, the best knowledge at the time insisted that I should clean the trees out of

19

the stream and remove flammable brush and woody debris from the forest floor. I started to do this in a beautiful cedar grove, but I spent too much time sitting on the ground looking at the trees—I suppose I could blame Artemis, goddess of forests, solitude, young girls, and the hunt, for possessing me—but looking was more rewarding than the labor-intensive "housekeeping." Somewhat later, scientific knowledge advanced, and I was advised to drop trees into the stream and leave all the woody debris and brush on the forest floor. Had I been less contemplative or lazy, I would now have much more work to do. Was what I did in the 1970s good? Is what I am doing now good? Do I need more training to determine what is good or bad? Is the failure to do the good of now, or then, bad? Have I failed from ignorance (conflicting knowledge) or from confusion (conflicting intentions)?

That is one problem with forestry or ecology between today. Which action is good? Which is bad? Which should we do? Unfortunately, the outcome of our exploitation or interference may not be evident for hundreds of years. Perhaps we should aim for harmony, for the health of forest and human communities.

I think that we should do good for one's harmony, for instance, or for the health of the forest, not because the action is an action or for the sake of doing something good. In doing, we choose between good and bad actions; the judgment makes us human and susceptible to error. Good forestry can do nothing more. Perhaps, as John Fowles suggests, all our judgments of good and bad are meaningless in the long run. All actions, good or bad, interweave so extensively as time passes that their individual goodness or badness disappears. Each becomes lost in the other. Judgments evaporate and landscapes remain. Even so, we must consider our actions and perform them, guided by notions of goodness and harmony.

Good forestry, creating good images and good goals, and good living in forested places, is concerned with resacralizing landscapes, with restoring them to their extents and grandeurs, by regrounding science in ethics (that is, ways of living together), and by changing our attitudes from utilization and flat efficiency towards awe and appreciation. That means that we, you, me, have to care for each tree, fungus, jay, sowbug, or worm. Each living being matters. We know so little about the lives of trees or of other beings; we do not know what it is like to live for over a thousand years or to stand in one place and draw everything we need into us. We do not know what it is like to live underground and browse between roots. We do not know what it is like to crawl through shrubs, although Gary Snyder suggests that we should try that more often. Our detachment from trees and other beings has to end. Our conscious and restrained participation in the life of the forest—in the life of any ecosystem—must begin. Poetry, especially works like *Eutopian Dreams*, shows the way.

The Altazor orchard under snow

Weeds

Walter and Bessie

Over the hill a white orchard
blooms over spring shadows;
weathered house long abandoned
over a fallen porch, the dining
room window black without glass.

Light moves, so I walk closer
hugging my sides for warmth
then press my face against
a surviving pane, hooding
my eyes, hand on a surface
of nonreflecting fluid, not
drinking—then the years repeal—
pushed forward from pain-etched
shadows, my father's face, wan,
remote from this green present
and mother's, lined from work,
gazing out the new window
towards what?—the grey
and shapeless future when
the house has passed to ruin
the furnishings to distant hands
and their essences reduced
to photographs?
—but not with bitterness,
with understanding.

The image passed, line by line:
What we create we cannot hold
but must let grow beyond.
The past closed up, the wind
stirred cherry blossoms.

Winona Stars

Late spring and the cycle was cresting
with a fresh troupe of players
and Winona, sensing the end of her act
yet holding the stage together
gathered light behind her eyes to express
the feelings left. Her hands composed
her eyes focused and flared
then dimmed and released their light.

We return the ashes but keep our hologram
images for memories. All her movements
were illuminated, her skin reflected light
and the caress of photons carried messages
to the stars. If we could overtake the waves
of light, we would find her standing in her
nightgown three years out, then sitting
on the porch with Joseph long past Centaurus
clowning with her children at forty years
distance, and once, beyond Arcturus, a sweet
maiden standing frozen in a garden for the first
photograph—the youth, the girl, the baby
moving outwards on expanding spheres of light
towards other galaxies. If we could somehow
wait eighty-two light years away and collect
the rays from earth in a lens of slow glass
we might see all her motions relived.

But, it would not be her. We have our memories
and we renew her through our lives. The troupe
is young, but adventurous and accomplished;
they play on a path with blue bachelor buttons
in a mist of light. It is almost summer.

Accomplishments

No one will make your house a monument
or put a marker at your place of birth;
there will be no great songs of fame—
no public recognition of your name.

What have your children ever done?
They never guided anyone by force
never tried to change or coerce
and they would always be hurt
rather than give pain in return.
They never piled up symbols,
and never tried living alone
for Art or God or Man—how
will they ever be known?
They never advertised themselves
or sold their way for money,
they worked no miracles, pushed
no claims to sainthood, just offered
kindness unnoticed, gentleness
unrecorded—and no importance
is paid to lives lived in balance
as well as they could be.

But this is enough for you, that
your all of children were good
that they gave and received help
to make the world a little better.

The Past is Only a Tool
(The Tinker's Dame)

Shallow, quick, muddy water
Wears away the rock that's weak
And shapes a marvelous canyon
Many thousands of feet deep,
Unevenly exposed, showing
Layered colors and textures.

The past is what shaped us
What brought you to me
What made you sensitive—
Does it matter what you
Did, does it matter how
You became—Would I make
You change that past?

Shall I curse the dirty water
That washed over you once
While marveling at the contours?
What has touched you has passed:
A sculptor's dirty hands, the tool,
The mold, the smelly clay,
A hundred nights of pain.
It is you who formed, and remain.

Come to me and let me
Marvel once again—

Did I Not Do That, Also?

What did he really do? Just went
someplace before anyone else.
Of whom the statue? He was allowed
to rule over men. Of whom the painting?
She wrote unwritten thoughts—
And him and her? The others?
They arranged colors in pretty patterns
adding more elements of noise
to form as they got older.
Then he found chemical combinations
that helped others to live better.
She administered to the sick
while slowly wasting away herself.
He invented instruments to see differently,
He made a means of moving faster,
She acted out her fantasies for others,
and they moved in groves of swaying limbs.

Did I not do these things, not
discover unseen places, not change
things with my presence,
not see the world was petty
as well as sometimes spring and pretty?
Did I not?

I fell with the leaves in fall,
I knew, I chose,
I died and rotted and rose
as worms and grass and dew,
as birds I flew
as rivers I ran and flowed
in trees I stood again
in paper, waves, and pen
I spoke
and so, I live in you
whole.

Remembering Decades

Every year, around the equinox
that measures the length of light
and measures the depth of my loss
a thought slowly rises in me
that you died on this day.
So every year I stop and think
that you could not—
I remember where you are
and remember where I was that day.

And this year I was on a mountain
wilderness lying on yellow grasses
watching clouds reform like fantasies
in water, feeling the mist on my face
and wondering how much higher
I could climb before light fades
and determines where I rest,
and I think: You could be here
with me, if you had not thought
that an hour's romantic brace
was more important than lying together
as one with the other, just beasts
beneath the sun and rain on a bed
of mosses and grasses—having collected
all the intervening days of listening
to other voices with other messages, other
attractions, distractions, and dreams,
and then conversed about them.

No one misses you like your brother
but I am only that and I was not there
to counsel your decision to die
and I only wait now, but I no longer hurry;
time is not mine any longer; in the depth
and chaos of the flow I am only an eddy
collecting experiences for both of us
a few thoughts and a few words
that I cannot release to anyone else.

The Nexus of Permanence

This moment no one sees
this moment only me—
if all my past were resurrected
if my mind dissected
if all those moments could be counted
and carefully amounted
the moments would be almost all of me—
is all my life not these?

When my eyes could not discern things
the walls and furnishings
recorded all that could be heard and seen
in the deep vibrations in their being.

The most magical moments passed unnoticed
unnoticed by anyone else
unappreciated, they were scattered
as sound as light in matter
in waves to the trees, rocks and stars
into walls and floors
recorded by the earth in murmurings.

I give myself to my surroundings
all the weight of life
all that came before, became me,
and I pass so easily.

Darkness Still

I love the darkness
and it loves me, I believe—
not the darkness of the earth's shadow,
but where light has never been,
in my heart, in my brain, between stars,
where galaxies have yet to go, in the emptiness
before anything was —

Lightbearer

    I absorb light
from the sun during
the day or at least
make it internal so
       it can carry taste
and sound. At night
release it so I can see

during the rare
    times I can shed
the verbal embrace
and not think or try to speak
I can still see. I am less
and less human
       the pulse of blood
quiets and slows

then I am dark
not as a shadow
    or the absence of light
but as dark as where
light has never reached
at the edge of being
       or in my heart.

Sweet Flowers Bitter Fruits

Other Lovers

So often, I have watched other lovers
And wondered who they used to love;
If not each other,
Then who?

Someone like me or someone like you,
Who found something more
With someone else
A while,

A different face and different smile
But not a kinder one or
More wonderful
Just one

That shined only on you, like the sun
That dimmed the stars by day
Until it, too
Grew cold,

Until you, too, had grown too old
To turn the last one away
And called him
Your love

Having forgotten that moment of
True feeling was mine—
Love that knew
No time . . .

The Place of Reconciliation

Sometimes I cannot wake you from your
Larval sleep
When I need to tell you
of a dream I had to
Wake to keep:
A rounded hill, overlooking Potlatch,
Grass still green,
We walk holding hands until we could
Not be seen
Then stylistically in slow motion drift
To the ground
And hold each other tenderly, tightly
Without a sound
Our history of troubles dissolved
By the dew
Evaporated by the sun and wind, carried
To a place
Where human concerns joined with those of
Other beings
Where feathers, furs, scales, and hair have no
Special meanings.
Filled with that feeling, we walked back,
I Forgave you
And I never thought of you again, dreamed or
Saw your face.

Dancing in the Dark

I saw you dancing by yourself
in a room half-dark with memory,
felt gravity loose its gentle bonds
and the earth slow down while you spun
wordlessly alone, almost unseen,
twirling around in a dream
flying away, you know, with me.

What music have you always carried so,
how many thousand miles ago?
Where would I look to find
the origin of that celestial motion
that keeps the footprints on the rug
two steps behind? I saw you
with your arms folded on your bosom
but ready to sweep any unwary
preoccupied man or record album
into your exciting embrace.

I saw your legs move through your skirts
I saw your hair unbound and flowing
I saw the light in your face.
How many times was this the joy's
only possible expression,
how often lifted you from depression
how often was all direction lost—
the entire world lost—
that you could discover the one within?

All the stars were spinning, and planets
and stones, falling leaves
waltzing in a whirl
turning to snowflakes in a swirl
in clouds spiraling like atom-patterns
dancing, and you,
and you.

Two Galaxies

A room
Aztec fruit in ice
in a China bowl. A bite
and history commences.

Like independent galaxies
through complicated courses
toward inevitable collision
we gather each other in
with irresistible forces
that grow as we move closer.

A pillow
sliding fingers
Arabian patterns intertwining
in an English carpet.

We have found these little ecstasies
in timid explorations
but we must crash like galaxies,
completely
flowing together
separate and distinct
with parts without division
welded and glowing as nuclear lines
are sent and strung between us
like communicating fires.
Bodies in unrestrained collision
swept from us like dust from stars
and planets, bound in hot desires
two distant galaxies colliding—
fall in, fall into me—

The warp and woof
of fine black wool
mirror the field of being
through every scale.

As we touch we change and grow
as our content changes
our pattern changes slowly too.
We never notice what was is gone
as our bodies rearrange
into something new.
We are each a focus of the universe
a nexus of collisions
with eyes that act like lenses
to enlarge the world we know.
Let the gaps fill in and spaces
meet around us—
    fall into me, fall in—

Sonnet 47 *Eidolon Lost*

Much whiter than the starlight on the snow
Your floating form beside me. Lighter flow
Your fluid movements than the dancing reams
Of particles from clouds where moonlights glow
And follow gliding patterns. And clearer seems
Each sparkling eye than any crystal streams
And in them truth that I might find and know
My lady made of dust from stars and dreams.

I wished, an instant, that you would be my lover
Though I knew that you would never love me
As a fleeting form that I could never hold
And I knew that I would rather not discover
That you are as free as the winds above me
And like the careless winds above me—cold.

What It Was Was

It was tired light on cracked plaster walls
While sitting quietly with you near
And reading or entertaining friends
On furniture we refinished.
It was cooking meals together
And going for aimless walks,
It was movement and direction,
It was coming home.

It was struggling with our problems
And working for better times,
It was being angry or sad
Or waiting to show you something
Or trying to hide something else,
It was laughing at ourselves—
It wasn't you I loved.

It was being warm under the blankets
And playing around in bed
Then stopping for a while.
It was being with you
And seeing you smile—
It wasn't you.

The sun room & back porch (from recycled grain- elevator wood)

Her Plea

By one sleeping body curled
Another sleeping near.
Your radiating body is my world
And my center is here.
So, like a desperate planet
Cast off from its sun
I try to find a closer orbit
By becoming one
Always facing you, always
Keeping warm.
From your leaving
I may die still shrinking
From my grieving
Losing confidence and thinking
It is far too far to another star—
Help me please, keep me
keep me always in your arms!

First Dream

I have bamboo over my bed
And sometimes in the darkness
I hold you, look over your head,
And pretend:
>   We are lovers
>   Hidden in the gold-green rushes
>   Past the fields by the water
>   And the buffalo drum hoof beats
>   Past timber houses to the river,
>   Driven by boys with bamboo sticks
>   Who splash around with shouts—
>   And waken you on the mud bank
>   To kiss me. No, it is late
>   And we must go for food, now,
Remember?

Aurum nostrum non est aurum vulgi

Little fires reaching through my arms
Reaching down my spine
You have fires too, as slow and
Eloquent as mine
And they move together separately
And meet, in time
Then time will disengage
And they will rage
And—oh—the joy of being consumed
Of having struggled so
And finally, fully bloomed!

Moments

You always meant to smile
You know it and you kept it secret
The joy that came through others.
You saved and hid away
Until you were all alone
That moment no one saw
That no one even knew existed
That moment you saved
For a time to be renewed.
And, someday, when you're old
And all the colors turned with age
You'll remember all the moments
And think that's all that ever was—
The moments all were you!

Why You're Bad for Me

If I have crumbs on my chest
And you brush them off,
I tend to be sloppy just
So you'll have to touch me.
If my hair is mussed
If my shirt untucked
Then I'm lost—
Being out of order around you is hopeless.
I want to be touched!

Why You're Really Bad for Me

I'm always out of breath
Around you. I can't control my heart
Or mind. I get a fever—
You're no relief.
I might just want
You to be worse.

The Wing of Your Eye

My eye, like a frog's
Sees only floating curves:
The arch of clouds in the sky
The wing of your eye-
Brow, the swerve
Of your lips, line of calf,
Tightness of foot, roundness
Of stomach, grace of breasts—
Every muscle a geometric
Perfection for my sight.
The arc carries my consciousness
Yet keeps it from disconnecting.

Microscopia: *The Bridge of Light*

At first glance the object shimmers on the plate
in a multicolored halo, as we thresh through light
to the hidden grain. The texture of everything is woven
with strands of light; it is light that joins the levels,
crossing all discontinuity. Light is the bridge
between the infinitely small and the infinitely large.
The galaxies are milk splashed on the dark;
yet when we splash milk to regard it under the lens,
we see galaxies of atoms. The stars speak light,
and if we could learn the words we would hear
the history of everywhere light has touched.

We live in a metaphysics of light, and we need
only gaze to our soaring cathedrals to be reminded.
We have created a chamber of forest filtered mists,
where the radiance of light is stained and dimmed
to fit our minds. When the red sun sets beneath
the sea, its last ray is green. Colors hide in white,
bursting out of the line. Green comes from burning.
We wait in the green night.

Plants must worship light; grasses shine, cowbells drip,
and the day's eye follows the sun across the sky.
Sun fire wakens the bud, and sun mists enter
the ear; sun time unfolds the calyx that sun fingers
open the petals; sun heat dries the leaves,
and sun dust bends the stem; sun wind carries
the debris. Sun life drives the world.

The sun is the heart of comets and planets,
as the heart is the sun of the body.
The sun quickens the heart of flesh,
and it becomes a heart of fire, our blood its light;
and the light of the sun and the light of the heart
meet in the mind. Light turns our abstractions
into a circle, from the harsh geometry of the sun to
the gentle touch of April. Meaning is hidden in light.

Wild Apples

Amaryllis

I saw you under moonlight and you
Reflected me. I saw you under starlight
And you grew distant and mysterious:
Your skin was the color of evening
As if you breathed that color in
And pumped the blood of sky through
Your flesh—your nipples were darker
Than your breasts—your hair a deeper
Blue—your eyes held aurora lights.

I saw you again in the forest by day
Standing under the cedars
Swaying before me in green—
Your body was a tender shoot
Nourished by the blood of leaves.
Your limbs were lighter than
Your body, as if newly grown
And your face about to bloom.

I held out my arms to you
But you turned and ran
And changed as you did:
Clay and dirt made you red and brown
Rocks on the cliff turned you grey;
You looked back once as you fell
Through air—

Bastet

Bastet—bewitcher, bewilderer,
Savior from evil spirits
And mistress of all who travel,
Goddess of the Nile,
I knew you by your style,
Your flavor of decadence
The knowing glance of permanence
When eons were brief to your smile.

Queen of all unanswered questions,
Much reposed in you
That will never be spoken or heard
And all your ambiguities
Are mystic prophecies.

How old are you, how old is water?
Was there water when you first awakened?
How many times has your timeless
Body been refined
By the river of forgetfulness?

When you were born
Was the moon aloft to call the tides
And release them to the shore?
Is it you who measures seasons
And intertwines them with her colors?

Who is it who carries clouds
In the blue of her eyes
Whose eyes are like planets
That turn and bear storms,
Who holds the green of papyrus
By her side and welcomes sunlight home?

Counting Universes

Orange peel tar glass rope wood—
We see only what is large enough to see
And because light strikes faster than we;
Moment to moment we see things—there
Under dead weeds, beneath a smile.

Moira danced on squeaky sand.
It was solid beneath her feet because
Its motion was greater than hers.
But we can't catch the feet that won't
Be caught or hold them in our net.

Warmly deposited, she fell asleep;
She dreamed and painted her dream:
Mushrooms parachuting to war,
Green sea cucumbers exploding
On a destruction-heated beach.

She found a single surviving shell
Heard the songs of drowned cities,
And the history of life in the sea.
She took it home to her kitchen drawer
(more than life itself we prize debris).

From broken rocks the water wore
The tide presented pieces she recognized:
Galaxies of stars on seaweed-flooded skies—
Once she saw a strange radiant fish
And sudden clarity—

The Ground

These leaves have fallen before
With a falling that is older
Than we who watch.
And this limitless falling
We see with a vision older
Than the falling itself.

When I touch you
The coincidence of having
Touched you those countless times
With the freshness of touching you now
Dehisces my body Into two overlapping leaves
One eternally repeating what
The other finds new for the first time
One speaking what little can be said
The other feeling what cannot
One touching the other touching
Both intertwining in spirals
About you.

To see is to see farther than the trees
Whose leaves have fallen into space before
Toward a ground that is older
Than our vision.

The Origin of Myth

Our bodies bend light, our love is like an egg—
Primordial cosmic ylem bound impenetrably in
One-way porcelain—
                       letting myriad senses enter.
But nothing returns to the universe
From whence it came,
Untransformed.
Our bond is of a kind
Not nuclear or chemical.
The glass may be inspected from without,
Creatures may curiously peer in
Or sink infinitely slowly in
If they get
Too close, but they cannot break in
And spread us out like spoiled fluid.
The egg could only rupture
If a tide
Of feeling were to separate us—
If the forces
Could not be balanced
                        —the egg would break
Our energy and pain would furnish substance
For those it intersected by its radiating
Sphere—our love become a myth.

The Clothes of Silence Laid Aside

I lay down	you lay down
we fell asleep	not touching
our thoughts	converged questioning
over the distance	the necessity of separation
the wind, cool air	lowered us into dreams
we touched pushed	down flowered sheets, we
trust the dreams	are strong

enough to hold us now

Perception Like Candlelight

She washes her face by candlelight,
No neon stage or fluorescent store
Just a single candle by the mirror.
A face that age cannot identify
In the gentle glow, nor tension flaw
The halo blending in comfortable darkness.
We see each other so—
With perception like candlelight.

The music room at Altazor Palace

45

Wild Apples

Aphrodite's Fruit
I picked the first apple
And received the name of the spirit:
Melus, melon-bellied Melus
Old priest of Aphrodite—remember?
The spirit of the tree reborn
In blossoms, consummated in fruit.
I polished it and held it up—
Reflections of a crow passing—
We broke it in half.

We picked the seeds from its core
Named them all each other
And threw them to the wind.
We floated down in slow embrace
Beneath a spreading tree
With branches reaching over
Like arms in benediction.
Below us it sent roots to trace
The heart of water.

There is a time of critical need,
There is a distance where bodies react
And a reaching toward critical mass
When all the rules change
And qualities become strange.
Boundaries decay with energy's
Conversion, saving, and release.

Cocoon of Light
Caresses caused phosphorescent mists
To rise above our heads.
The sun spun sheets of light
To cover our delicate flesh.
The light became thicker
And dropped as we quickened
And made a cocoon with its threads.

We suffered the weight of moments
As if all time had stopped
And the past collected and pushed
Until all space had burst—
Sweet, golden, amniotic net
All twisted bindings come undone
Then tighter round again
Sticky, silky, shining skin.

Oh, that we clawed weakly
Not wanting out too soon.
Muscles tensed, stretched,
Jumped, and then collapsed.
The hands became heavy and slow
The hands became heavy and held;
The eyes became heavy and closed.

Dream of Dionysius
In the morning three apples were picked
From the tree of knowledge
And brought to him for his meal.
He turned one in his hand,
The two sides of the apple
Were faces of the moon
One invisible, one visible,
The secret of life and death.

She carried three apples as gifts
From the tree of life.
He understood their meaning
And ate— The fruit dropped from a tree,
Leaves turned and fell, as did he—
The body was burnt on a pyre
Whose flames returned to the sun.

I lay on my back, looking up
Through nine radiating branches
At the dappled sun. I gazed on your face
As smooth as the moon of day

47

And on your white-limbed body.
I loosened your hair and put
An apple in the hollow of your hand;
The other held absence of poppies.

From Umbriel Observed
The crust of light lay shattered;
The sun cracked in the sky.
We lay touching in grass
Our hands clasped at our sides.
We are as we were before, unless—

We have been tempered by our burning.
Emotions have their gravity
Attracting more around them.
We are a focus of particles
From everywhere. The energy
Of motion concentrates in us
Until we cannot hold it in—
Explode
And rise beyond the clouds and out.

The orchard is a galaxy of trees
Then it is gone. There is nothing
But clouds and whirls of blue and brown,
Vapor trails from the earth and moon.
We rush outward on a wave of light
Passing the wrecks of asteroids.
The stars coruscate like blossoms
In a field of black. Looking backwards
From the limit of light we see
The dwindling bright circle
Like a polished apple
Whose red heat hides the white interior.

With Locust Flowers

Your kisses were scented with locust
but held the poignancy of fall
only I know it wasn't that way at all.

Your body was petal-smooth to touch
and opened like a day in spring
only I know that it wasn't anything

like that—your honeyed kindness
smothered me like summer heat,
only I can't remember what

happened afterwards
and the caterpillar winter is coming
and I have no hint of—

October Light

I opened the curtains, brushing
brown Celtic patterns;
you lay down.

I opened the window and turned
and stood still while you
closed your eyes.

The wind brushed your hair as
you were falling asleep.
I saw it.

The sun touched your cheek when
you rolled on your side.
I heard you sigh.

Wind and sun and memory held you
so you could not move.
I only wanted to—

Ille Terrarum

Ille terrarum mihi praeter omnis Angulus ridet — Horace
[That corner of the world smiles for me more than anywhere else]

I cannot love you without the scrawk
of bluejays, without the approval
of coyotes we know
by name,
without the comfort of the land,
without the rising and setting of the sun
to align us, without the ceremonies of corn
and grapes, without the help of shadows
and planes
and the hundreds of webs and lines and ways.
I cannot love you for long if the roots
are gone.
Your sacred touch, untied,
is not enough;
we are not strong enough, alone.

Failing Sleep

Nocturnis ego somniis iam captum teneo — Horace
[in my dreams sometimes I catch and hold you]

I lie awake and dream of you
I wake and dream of you
I dream of you.

I dream and what I dream is past,
then I wake and what I see is past
and when I dream and wake suddenly
then I have you—briefly.

No position is complete
the goal of sleep: to catch and hold you
I lower to dream again.

Just a Smile

When God made me he put essences of other beings
into me: A piece of wolf, a bit of crow, a few needles
from a pine tree, a spot of fungus, some worm,
chunks of rock, a little beetle wing, whatever else
was lying around. Then, I enjoyed being with all
my relatives, and I was at home wherever I was.
But then I loved you and you made me more
human, so much so that I neglected the other
connections—almost forgot them. We kept
to the concrete city and exclusively human
things. We celebrated human differences
and human heights, but then you left me
for a simple human being—you told me to go.

So now I live with real people—owls and lizards,
grasses, coyotes, lichen—without you. I remember
them and yet I have not forgotten you or the time
I was almost dead. I run quietly through the night;
I am ruthless. I lick the blood. I sit and fumble
through the soil, empty and full, shredding bark
and twigs, tasting the not-quite-sweet cambium.
I open under the sun, extending tendrils down
between roots, between diatoms and water
drops. At last my shredded spirit is diffuse; maybe
it will never return, but maybe it will never need to.

Now, Spokane has crushed you and you need me
and I have come to help you, but when I show
my teeth, are you sure it's just a smile? When
I caress your head, when I explore your fingers,
is it because you were my mate or just my prey?

Leaving Palouse

Driving west at sunrise on highway twenty-six across
the Palouse hills
As I go down every hill the sun sets in the east
and as I go up every hill it rises again,
blinding me in the rearview mirror.
I lose track of time because it seems like I have been traveling
for days. The days all look the same,
and I know that they are—
these are the very same days that I traveled ten,
twenty, thirty years ago.
A different memory greets me on each slope:
a flat tire there, a picnic here, the day I raced a Jaguar
to the city limits
(the Subaru made the corners better),
the night I missed a corner and ended up in a ditch
poised for take-off, looking at the stars wink
their light-years-late hellos,
and knowing two glasses of wine were waiting
for me on the table.

August brown bunchgrasses wave good-bye
and my tires hiss their reply. Shadows lead the way,
dark fingers pointing from dark pools. A redtail hawk
watches from a fence post satisfied that things are right.
Only a sun-dried sagebrush blocks my way
and it is not enough to deflect the momentum of a hundred
bad decisions and wrong turns.
If I thought I could turn back time with each ascent
and backward-setting sun I would drive until the hills
were eroded flat, and every one but me had given up
and was still,
but the car keeps moving smoothly
and the illusion of progress fools
the tired, emptying mind.

Knowing Why

I've learned a few things (not that many, though).
I know why the leaves fall in October and I know
why the gopher snake bites when you pick him up.
I know why water runs downhill and where it goes
and I know why an owl flies and the lichen grows.

> The leaves fall because the maple protects
> itself from the dark and cold, and a snake bites
> because he doesn't know you or your intention.
> Water seeks a resting place, a stable situation,
> and the owl has to catch her food, and lichens
> are trying to split every barren rock open.

But don't ask me why you left me—did you need
to protect yourself? Did you not know me? Did
you need a place to rest where I would not pester
you? Were you hungry or did you just need to
degrade me? I don't know. I really don't know why.

> But, I do know that now I am more at home
> with snakes and owls, squirrels and lizards
> than I ever will be with your ambitious
> neglect. I know why a coyote howls, but not
> why I must learn to. I know why a lion hunts
> and rests alone, but not why I continue to.

I don't know why some swans don't mate for life
while others do. I don't know why some wolves
never mate and others do. I know why I want you
for life, but I don't know what you want—
I don't know and I know you can't tell me—
and I worry that it's too late, but I don't know why.

Altazor Forest Passage

I don't tell anyone where I am, just
like I didn't tell anyone there where
    I was going. Now, I'm in the forest, but
I'm not alone, no, everyone here has heard
me stumble through the brush and vines,
but they let me go my own way. The painted
turtle couldn't escape and had to be held,
as unwilling as you but easier to catch. He
showed me the direction to the stream.
The bull snake path pulled my gaze to
the berries that were old but very sweet.
    I poked into the old dry leaves that crinkled
with his passage—never did see him.

Fir trees protect me from the sun;
a breeze winds around me exhausted
from forcing its way past the edge
trees' low boughs, but welcome and scented.
A chipmunk scrambles out of reach
along a log, certain that I'm hungry
    for her—and only her flesh.
Across the sky, the eidolons flirt
before turning into merely clouds
    that whirl into other shapes.
Birds sing and let me know when
someone's coming so I can hide as well.
Turkey buzzards patrol the whole
forest just above the treetops.

I'm not upset, I'm not afraid, the harm
that's possible is not the cruel kind.
Bear rambles along, leaving berry-rich
piles of dung; I poke it with a stick
    to see if it's still warm. It is.
Now it's dark, I walk through the trees
    just slightly darker than the deer
trail slightly darker than the sky beyond.
A mountain lion watches without giving

away her position—I know because I smell
her slightly stronger than the leaves.

Every passing moment something human
slips away from me like night fog.
I am incapable of feeling, although
I can move quietly like a lion
through the needle-dry trees.
I am as cool as the moss that grows
    over old logs. I am as dark
as the soil under decayed wood.
I am as content as the black bear with
the richness of fall berries. Every day I close
myself a little more to useless information.
    Soon I will be incapable of speech.

The Altazor orchard from the bedroom window

Fragments

Aeakus Humbled

You had perfect wings
silken, new, ten-ribbed, white—
we tore them off—
on the cinder path
under cavernous air.
You cried but could not move
in the absence of wings.

You had perfect eyes,
blue—no gold—and piercing—
they could make us move
or burn ours out—
we tore them out
. . . left you under the bridge
by the river of oblivion.

"Mother, father, crippled judges
can you take away my perfect heart?"

Tantalus

The [citrus] rolls and falls off
the table and rolls under it—
the thought retreats.

We reach for particles and stars
and they recede beyond our grasp.

Everything is made of particles
full of strangeness and [charm]
that we cannot possess.

Trees lift fruit beyond our reach
and water recedes from our thirst—
it is our desires that offend.

Antaeus and Herakles

Dusty hero approached dusty hero
along a dusty road—at
first equally matched
sinews popped and sweat ran.

But Antaeus drew his strength from his mother
the earth and slowly [prevailed] against
his opponent with a laugh. Herakles was bent
backwards until, almost broken, he thought—

He swung and lifted Antaeus off
the ground and choked him as his strength
grew feeble, the strong limbs wilting in air.
Water conquers earth.

You are our nemesis, Herakles,
for you are strong enough and cunning
to separate us from the source
of our strength, the earth.

But we are Herakles as well, and strangle
ourselves, punished by the gods
for our pride in individual power.
. . . [now] fire waits.

Odysseus

I was under contract to a truth
I did not know. I fought great battles
With myself . . . purified myself
With violence and longing.

All things have been wedded in memory
And the source of all these, you,
Telemachus and even Argus. I had
To journey home, a symbolic journey
Like that of birds in a cage.
Home can only be approached from [a] distance
. . . spiraling around the center,
Returning, reordering the chaos of choice.

I spent years in Circe's bed. I left
After exhausting everything but the memory
Of home. I long for home and comfort
And death.
My faith is such that even burdened [with age]
And wrinkled, I will plant seedling trees.

Penelope

. . . shall be not Odysseus we praise
but Penelope, not the adventurous braveteer
but the woman constant and clear
. . .
not he who takes exceptions, not he
who ever roams, but the [keeper] of homes,
the center . . .
not inspiration, not the prodigal son,
but she who perseveres
not one marvelous action, not the sudden
tide, but the river flowing and calm,
the water steady and near . . .

Children of Ankaa

We dream of darkness
And build buildings without windows.
We fear fire
And bury our dead in bronze and stone
Remembering what Heraklitus
Saw in the hearth—
The spirit of the forge, defender
Against beasts and [the] cold
And dark, but, too, our possible
Annihilation beyond bones.

Our oldest myths are myths of the sun.
We have memories of perfect forms
And abstract them still
From cloudy images.
We long to see ghosts in metal
And powers of healing in trees.

We are fascinated by the myriad faces
Of [energy] and court their embraces
In our searching.
The earth is our body and our body
A burning house—our blood is red
With heat, our skin the color of ashes.
We are the ashes of stars;
When we are dead
Who knows what will rise.

Heraklitus's Dream

The earth turns; sun lights forests
and fields, and they breathe;
[matter] feels.

Pines transform light to [sugar].
Then the earth turns from the sun
and the forest exhales.

Leaves disappear in flames
invisibly, radiating heat at night.
The forest is a burning house—
whole mountains burn coldly,
more slowly than stars.

Life is fire, and it does
not need a body of its own;
it dies and is reborn in everything.

We live by the interior touch of flame,
tenuous flame, dissolving weight;
fire is the [thing] in bloom.

Phoenix

You were born on the wind from burning day
Your wings and feathers from shafts of light
Your beak obsidian, your talons shards of ice
You only—there could be no other.

You flew [aloft] for hundreds of years
Alone, not wanting [not] needing rest.
You searched the desert for hundreds more
For the palm to build your nest.

From aromatic limbs you wove a pyre
And waited for the fire to rise.
You preened your crimson plumage
And rested your ancient eyes.

You shrilled an alien song:
The sun's rays focused—ignited a root.
You fanned your wings and uttered cries
As the palm tree burned with its red fruit.

Calm companion of heat, you know
the complexion of flames. You rose
from genetic ashes feathers fired,
a spectrum from the white.

You will live as long as the sun
Setting and rising from the palm
The same yet new until there is nothing
Left but the palm in blackened skies,
Then the ashes will cool, the song will end.

The Shadow of the Mistress of the World

It is the way—all movement turns to heat.
You burn and rise from the ashes.

As the phoenix burns the wind stirs
The ashes and rises—
The sky darkens with torrential rain
But the [helix] turns, the code remains.

The ashes expand and steam; something
Moves and fights its way out—
Dark nebula—
Molten red metallic bird renewed.

Particles burn, particles fuse
Fire phoenix, you grow
Wood, earth, metal phoenix.

You grow and your shadow grows
Still larger. Order and [heat]
Create complexity in ashes.

Your feathers are now metallic
You alter yourself to survive
But only you notice the change
And the change is irreversible.

How much of your life does
The shadow take as its own?

The Others

"When he recalled his first home and the wisdom there,
And his fellow prisoners in that time, don't you suppose
He would consider himself happy for the change and pity
The others?"

Platon, *Republic* VII 516e

The world is washed with light; sky and rock
Are bleached white. There is the sea
And the faded green of trees.

To be as you taught, we thought we advanced
Toward perfection, but we became weary and lost—
Our tongues dried out. We perceived nothing
But intervals of light. We could not reach
Your ideal. . . . [nor] erase our origins.
You called us strange prisoners bound by our legs
And necks before shadows cast on the side
Of the cave by fires. You thought you freed
Us and dragged us up a rough, steep path.
You forced us to see the sun, source of the seasons
And steward of all things in the visible world.
From there we were led to contemplation of
What is best in the things that truly are.

But when we recalled our first home,
We longed for a world without weather,
Away from relentless, sun-driven change.
We longed to escape the weight of truth—
And then we found the cave again.
Let the hills take that unbearable mass
From our shoulders. Let the damp restore
Moisture to our skins and the dark
Return our dreams.

The abyss opened under our feet;
All we wanted from you, Platon, had not
The power to raise us higher—the dialectic
Does not lead upward, or outward;

There is no up or down, in or out,
Only the continuing spiral onward.

Where is the architect of the cave,
Whom we once praised? Welcome us back
With new designs. Make walls to keep
The sun from our eyes. We will use shadows
And mirrors to freeze its awful visage.

This is the place of life—the caves
Are not vacant, as the plains above.
We have made the earth secure with our
Own dark geography, comfortably bound.
This is our fathers' hearth. Savor
The aroma of cooking lamb—the senses
Expand—hear the trickle of water seeking
Its level through chiaroscuro rooms.

The caves are home. In filtered light
We polish the walls lustrous . . .
Ordained in the wombs of our mothers
To sow doubt in the entrails of the earth.
We meditate in the depths and sleep
In the [narcotic] knowledge of rock. Mysteries
Leak into dreams inverted in negative infinity.

We press the limits of darkness down
To the limits of our illusions, insert
Ourselves in crevices of being—[matter's]
Center and the heart's, invisible.
We burrow in the [solidity] of rock
And build temples to feeling.

You taught us that the activity of art
Had the power to release us,
But art has its roots in darkness
And though its surface is displayed
For all, it seeks to intertwine things
With invisibility that we may see them.
We must play with shadows and live between

Perfect light and darkness, a double life.
This is the true song of the dialectic
Weaving voices into silence and twining
All things opposite around an empty center.

The sun impales forms; their colors
Are burned off. Light decomposes flesh
And only proud skeletons remain.

Wisdom is a wild thing like the Arcadian doe
And not easily captured with words. The dappled
Form leaves its shadow in our grasp while it slips
Away undaunted. A hunger we do not understand
Keeps us on the scent. We cannot give up the chase—
Nor can we ever catch her. [So] to be wise,
We must act as if the shadow is the doe.

Daphne

. . . from the laurel your body bends
towards me, your arms like vines
wrap me and root me in the earth.

The chase is reversed and we become
human at last . . .

Authentic Fragments of Leukippus

1.0   The universe is composed of particles
1.0.1   The particles are all identical

1.4   Particles are forms (eidola)
1.4.2   . . . only think of how they are and call our
                  thoughts ideas of forms
2.2   Nothing is not the black shadow on the river bottom
                  nor the darkness lying in caves . . . not any object
2.2.3   . . . empty . . . undefined and featureless

3.1   Particles play into nothing

11.11   The secret geometry of chaos cannot be described
                  by any order nor simplified by names or numbers
                  nor reduced to particles in the void
5.11.3   The wild sky sings . . . the air and light . . .
                  not [simple] colliding particles . . . chaos lives!

8.12   Things are a pattern of particles
                  life is a pattern of things
                  thought is a pattern of life,
                  and the soul is . . . [pattern of thought]

9.7   There are no goals in life . . . no heights to be
                  attained once; there is only balance in relation

9.8   Life is not a preparation for death . . . it is an
                  experiencing of . . . patterns . . . The music
                  is played not saved for the end

12.6.3   Heraklitus asked me yesterday about the truth. I
                  replied [that] it depended on whether we were
                  walking under trees or through a river.

12.9   The injured Vulcan became armorer to the gods,
                  indispensable . . . are specialists [all] crippled? . . .

13.2   To jump into a volcano is not the act of a god . . .
but to return is . . . [and] who has seen
Empedokles lately?

13.4   The gods evaporate like clouds
they came from nothing and left nothing
behind, not thrones or texts or ruins or treasures—
what man now petitions their return?
If we exist in the image of our creators
then we are [but] clouds

21.1   We lose ourselves in images . . . burn our [brains]
with their brightness emitting blasts of sparks
that fade . . . the best turn to cinders in days.

24.0   Where are these theoretical particles?
where is the evidence of things not seen?
the substance of the hoped for . . . in the mind?

26.2   Let the caduceus be our symbol
as mystery is based on knowledge based
on mystery . . . through all levels
in an ever-recurring spiral

27.0   Ecstasy is a heart which the sun distends

28.0   One records the most profound meanings
the most ecstatic visions clumsily . . . occasionally
in fragments

Fossil Light

Small, Dark Windows

High on sacred mountains
Alone and cold, but dedicated
I have stood in the quiet night
And measured the purity of light
with collectors, bits, and numbers.

I have seen colossal stars reduced
To abstract points by distance,
Their colors bleached to white,
Yet thread the void with light
To tie the ends of darkness.

Each star sends a sphere
In every direction—here
Is only one penumbral point.
Space is crossed with light in lines;
The limits of our vision make night.

The universe blazes with radiation
From the hearths of its creation
Of trillions of stars—we see sparks
Through small, dark windows.
What drives stars and then departs?

Dark Moon

The sun and moon double-bodied
By chance by size and distance
Eclipsed by our perspective—
Reflection and its source imposed.

The earth and moon double-bodied
Turn over and over and over
In the plane of the planets
Exchanging light.

The sun and earth double-bodied
Behind the moon
Scatter bright seeds that
Bloom in space.

Binary

Slowly spinning in a symmetry of strength, carbon star
and iron star dance about a center, offering helium blooms
between them in a pulse of light. They give themselves
and grow. If things break the balance of attraction,
If some catastrophe pushes us apart that force
would destroy me, dissipating my body into the cup
of space, wasting the structure of millions of years
of careful evolution—my face radiating away—
Colors change from straining, structures fall, rush
inward, and explode, the fragments condense
Around a core from a sphere of light expanding—
Light wild light—The star becoming denser, burning
brightly for a time, remembering never to grow, never
to hold companion, never to rage, never exchange—
But the core, compacted tightly by gravity
Will burn so long a time, so constantly, ever so
constantly, gradually dying, ashes showing,
Dimly glowing, all heat remaining,
slowly, slowly going.

Moscow Mountain Light

He stands by the window outlined faintly
by starlight; on the other side of the glass
a thousand bright stars hang over
the mountains. Only from his small center
do the mountains seem more lasting
than the stars.

He does not move; behind him in a small
mirror starlight is doubled around
his shadow.

A small universe opens behind his eyes
and he fills it with stars.

The stars over the mountain
change subtlely. The shell
does not move.

There are things about light
that we cannot measure— joy
when we see the colors of sound,
things about being together
that we cannot name—
running through the woods
at dawn.
Each word is a piece of memory
and memory a piece of living—
you die and I live on.

Black Sun Waiting

The Longbeach sun came up black
And waited in the sky. You stepped
From the loft and waited on
The stairs. I turned in my sleep and
Faced that way, waiting for the moment
Light would join us from the sun—
You stepped down, my eyes opened—

Oh, Maen, do you realize how many
Reflections from the sun turned that
Very second—through space, reflected
From the particles of dust, from the clouds,
From the ocean, from the houses painted
White, from dunes almost as bright,
Through air, but changed, the light
Came through glass, thousands of simple
Messages through reddened curtains
Reflected from redwood walls from the
Quiet loft from the blue blanket from
Your pale body moving soundlessly
Down the stairs to my eyes open
Just that very instant—Do you?

I turned in my sleep
From houses painted white, from you—

Contemplating Speech

Five old people sit at a wooden
table, in the Moscow Hotel.
Thin, veined fingers peck
food, eyes locked in a shell
of memories of earlier days,
sorrow and happiness distilled
to masks—but through the eyes
the pure distance of dim
corridors once seen brightly
from the other end.
All the thin fibers bear light,
the fibers of the body, the nerves
with a spring to spread and reach
the sun inside. Their breathing
ruffles paper napkins on the table.

All that is best in order parallels
our breathing, insistent, framing
the house around new rooms. The heart
may tie us to life, but breath
is its rhythm and essence.
How can we say death is taking
place when life is being completed?
We do not finish all at once
but having the ability to speak
explain the circumstance of dissolution
and admire the miracle of speech—
reverberating through the fibers
an ageless delight settles in the flesh.

Amphibian Dreams

Lilith

We hear your voice moan over Ur,
Harrapan, Fatehpu and Tikal,
Daughter of night.
Created simultaneously
An opposite made, but undominated,
The ideal of the dream
Too equal for Adam,
You flew from his stubbornness
To an unjust punishment.

Come from your ruined cities,
Consciousness of night,
Show us your benevolent side—
We have learned to trust our instincts, now
And will not be confounded by reason.

Release us from the single vision
Of civilization. Shatter the wall
And reconcile us with Nature,
Oh, mind of the wild.
Return the idols to the soil,
Be midwife for our rebirth
And help us return to the sensual earth.

Throw your power on the side of the low
Until wholeness is restored, open
The gates of empathy, let it mingle
With creativity. We open our hearts
To your spirit, Lilith.

Three Nights in the Heart of the Earth

Beneath the melilotus and the bee trembling
Over it, in the bright archegonium
Of ideas, the mind impregnates the object.

The seed is lost under clay and rock.
We forget the now not present, once of such
Importance. What we watch disappear
Our children will not ever know, or miss
As we did not miss what our parents forgot.
All poorer in experience.

Centuries end like nights; all things vital
Wear away, until the core is exposed.
The world slips in and out of focus
To human eyes as they age. The seed begins
To germinate, using its inheritance.
It develops in its coat: the meristem
Divides, and the leaf primordia intends.
It sends its roots to rock, where light
Dwells between grains.

View of Altazor Forest from the back porch

Alone in a World of Wounds

We murder in ignorance or by accident,
A thousand ways in a thousand moments—
Every footprint leaving waste behind.

We kill for food or for convenience—
All living creatures feed on living;
Every hunger writes an autobiography
Of death. Our reverence is only
Acknowledgment of its necessity
And the fear of its consequences for us.

Our consciousness leads us from the whole;
That is how we know—in parts;
And that is its penalty. We must learn
Respect for iron, weeds, and flies
And grasp our way back.

Our obligation is to allow everything
That can to exist, not to control, promote
Or extinguish, but let each thing reach
Its full development.

Our duty is to feel, not transform or save,
To live, not evolve or finish, to respect
That the whole may feel in its diversity.

Our destiny is to turn the wheels
Of mortality and be turned under
Ourselves, that the earth may turn.

The Metaphysics of Order in Viola

The candles of the pines have all turned down
In the cold; the evening torrents
Through the needles, and a porcupine
Chews the tender bark.

The dead fir shoulders the sky, bones
Extended—a woodpecker thrills
The air with her ax. As the sun moves,
Shadows move and reveal that the tree
Has no front or back.

Cattails line the edge of the pond;
The earth vibrates as it turns
And the surface trembles. The movement
Of air circulates with the memory of all
The revolutions of the earth. The fish
Are still in their constant water.

The droppings of a bear point up the hill
But no bear is seen.
Gophers make honeycombs in dirt. Coyotes
Bark and burrow to the roots of heat.
A deer is surprised leaving the field
Where winter wheat suffer the delirium
Of weeds. The last geese pass; some absent.

White hills invade brown, snow settles
On the meniscus in the pail disguising
The waste of life. The field stretches and curves,
Folded and folded over, drifting with motion.
Crystal white hills frame a small white sun,
Glowing faintly on the horizon, packed
With crystal lattices—the field folded around
It. Memory complicates light around the star
And hills and draws them into another whole,
Smaller and dreamlike.

Signs

I.
A log had been destroyed—torn apart by claws—
Scat with prune pits surrounded the prune tree.
One afternoon a shadow—fifty-gallon-barrel
bear-size—crossed the edge of the field.
This morning, an apple tree was shredded.

II.
A tribe of deer stare at my trailer
lit up on a moonless night.
One challenges me: Are you whole?
Can you be this complacent in the snow?

I stare at them on the edge of the circle
until a frog croaks underneath the floor.
They are gone.

III.
The mountain bluebirds came back
one last time in November
to check the fencepost
for next year.

No one noticed them pass
the store or saw them
from Highway One so
invisibly they fly.

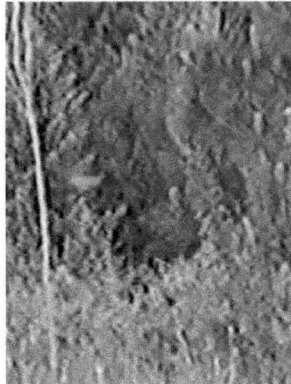

Neon hunting

Sea Anemone and Crab

> *I was at home*
> *And should have been most happy—but I saw*
> *Too far into the sea, where every maw*
> *The greater on the less feeds evermore.*
>
> Keats

I had thought all beasts alone, against
The world—but chimpanzees cry warnings
To antelope; satisfied wolves walk among elk,
Where all elk allowed a part to nourish
The wolf stomach that takes a share
From microbes within, to sustain blood
At whose centers live strange beings,
That can burn without ending.

The invader is conquered and tamed
Until the two live in dependency,
Two beings making three in a community
Of one—no one lives alone. Lichen
Break rock. Bacteria live at the roots
Of peas, and peas can dissolve iron
And build prairies.

The hermit crab claims a shell
To which a sea anemone attaches,
Protecting the crab with poison nettles
And feeding on the bits of leftovers.
When the crab moves, he takes his plants.

All nourishes all in a cycle
Of renewal—incomprehensible.
Destruction feeds the ecstasy of creation—

The Way of the Deer

There is a way of knowing
That is the way of the deer.
You will realize you know it
That you are already like
And unlike the deer
In feeling and thought.

The deer embodies experience;
The vitality and wisdom of
Her body ruins complete rationality
And loosens up our categories—
No monster Pan,
But a small being
Pleased at fitting between
The woods and fields so well.

How can you browse grass or rub
A tree without becoming it?
Dizzy with eating, exposed,
She scratches the surface
Of wholeness with her hooves,
With her green eyes.

Deer on restored skid road

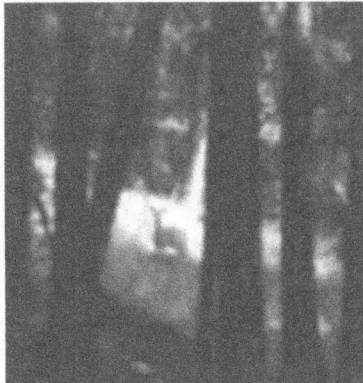

Wolf

I am wolf.   I chase the deer who chase the grass
who chase the sun. Grass is light, deer is light, wolf
is light, all is light. Across asia, siberia, america, europe,
I chase deer and mice and light. Not alone, no, always
with a family, always at home.

                                  I was raised by my parents,
uncles, aunts, brothers, sisters, and friends. I learned
cycles of heat, the meanings of clouds, the scent of prey,
the feel of grass—the culture of our ways: how to play,
and hunt and play. I found a mate, we played, shared
mice and moon and fluid—our way of mating is beyond
you—we lock and turn and we hold and hold until
we are dry and fall apart. We made a den; cubs came
from us and we joyed in their presence, teaching them
how to play, how to find food and eat, play and sleep
and play and play.

                       We were many, a populous people,
until your kind came with sharper teeth, faster claws,
greater numbers—many, many more—and took
our homes, our places, our food. There were fewer
places, fewer pups, fewer of us, then almost none—
and light has lost so many of its facets.

                                        I am wolf.
I am old and stiff. I need to piss—
ah, howl with me one more time for the missing
and the unborn, for lost worlds and lost light—
now, howl!
          (chorus)

Wolf News

This is what I, wolf, see: tracks, lines, bent
stalks, small prints in dirt—but there
are primary trails: vapors, clouds of smell,
the history of all who passed before me, their mood
and direction, health and intent, messages
that cannot go unread, only evaporate and be replaced
by newer ones, layer upon layer of deep rich
sediment, exhalations, urinations, oils, saliva,
hairs, excretions, the signs that let me taste who
ranks, who rejects, who mates, or not, who travels,
who kills, who sickens, who is at home, who is not,
whatever is dropped, brushed, torn, left behind,
whatever can be carried by wind and air and can tell
me the story of the hour, whatever I can use
to complete my own needs and understanding,
though there are things I do not know—
how do butterflies die? Do they just land, fold
their wings and wait, not to fly again? Does time
slow, or being extend? My own death
may not be as easy, but you can taste
that story later.

Shadow Play

Wolf folds
            shadows
around his shape to move quietly—
but the shadows remain
a few moments longer
                        for me to see.
The air adjusts slowly
to his absence.
                A shadow plays
with its source   with the observer;
        the forest hides
the shadow, the air
above the grass anticipates its form—

Wolf Loves to Hide

Nature loves to hide
   and nature loves to play

Play at hiding
      hide at playing
   Display
show and turn
and expect you
to remember.

   We remember
even as we see
again and the present
expands.

Nature loves to hide and tease
   wolves love to seek
humans love to seek and please

And so we seek each other and play
   and hide within nature
our nature   her nature   his nature
all the natures that exist.

Legend of Altazor

82

Convolutions

How the levels of salt and water have changed;
   Which streams lead to winter plankton;
      What canyons too deep, what volcanoes to avoid;
       Where the floating shadows came to destroy;
And where the temperatures rise and food is scarce;
   Where cascading rivulets excite flippers
     And tumble the body until the cold
       Awakens the need to surface.

Songs, songs for saving thoughts of wiser,
   Farther-traveled individuals or tasting
      Great adventures—history of thought in sound—
      Beauty of speaking them again. Songs
For entertaining, for mating—giving
  Of sperm and air, for expressing the intricacy
    Of balance, for creating fluid ideas
      That crest and evaporate in spume.

The invention of stories to explain the working
  Of waves and the purpose of breathing,
    Indeterminacy of water, the strangeness of air
And its relation to death, the substance
       Of other intelligent beings—the role
        Of reason to mold the universe
         And increase it.

Bear Masks

Bear masks, elk masks traced
On the wall of the cave.
We put on their skins and faces
To learn how they behaved.
They were kin and we needed them
As they needed wolves and men.
We took only the weakest,
The sick and old. Their strength
Was ours, we would not let
It ever diminish or grow cold.

Now the elk are silent, photographs
Show only hide and not the motive.
The real face is never seen. And men
Kill the strongest for trophies
And dismiss our art. The image
Of the elk is seen on metal cans
In the stream—The image
of the bear on boot polish.

We saw strangeness and sanctity
Not the human stink on every feature.
The bear was our father, elk helped
Us to be human. We changed
Ourselves to fit the earth. We fit
Ourselves to please the earth.
You will share our fate—faster
Now in ignorance full light.

The Cave of Night

She lay on her side,
Indifferent in sleep
Slowly music, and light
Dancers around a fire
One held up a metal disk

She woke, gazing at the wall
Its smoothness dissolved
As from acid on a copper
Sesterce—Vespacian's profile
She blinked
Redimensioned.

The smoothness was scored with scratches
As she watched
Scratches outlined figures sharply
Across a fissure
Altamira, the code of mystery
Renewed in red.
The deer are running.

Goodbye Fall

Little bluebirds, it's late October,
please fly back to me now
for an hour. I cannot wait a year
for your return. I will be underground by then.
My life is shorter than yours.
So please fly back and say goodbye properly
So I can breathe your beauty
one more time, and speak the silly human names
I gave you: Neon, Fric, Frac, Skymir, Vanity.
Hurry, I cannot wait to see your two-tone bodies
and hear your bouncy chirping song—I realize it will be
no different than the year that Fric
did not return to the house
on the trail—that is how life is filtered,
just not return one year.

Forest Light

Weeds

The capsule drifts in the wind over ruined earth
Descends with its sphere of hairs extended.
It rests abandoned; the wind whips dust around it;
      Rains drive it into a crevice.
It waits with millions of seeds from previous
Years, suspended for the right
Combination of temperature, moisture, depth,
      And light.
Seizing the moment, a ragweed appears
That thrives in heat and drought.
Five thousand seeds burst from it, it perishes.
      Ragweed colonizes the ground.
Then the field is a realm of ragweed, dandelion,
Lupine, foxtail, mustard, mullein, and salsify.
      The earth is bound in roots; winds
Cannot scatter it or waters waste it.
Dying weeds cover it and keep it moist.

Grass

In the shade of ragweed, cheatgrass and bromus thrive
And crowd the pioneers out.
      The grasses bind
The earth tighter in systems of roots, like skin.

Trees

After fifteen years, a pine appears
With heavy seeds and promise of a forest.

The Lives of Weeds

A weed is an unwanted plant, invader,
cheater, destroyer, thing identified by
a derogatory name: bindweed, stinging
nettle, prickly lettuce, ragwort, puncture
vine, thistle, the enemy of all that is valuable
crowding, robbing, carrying diseases
and poisons to humans, animals, other
plants—a problem to be annihilated.

Snapdragon, fleabane, ragweed, the most
productive of plants. The seeds—dandelion,
milkweed, thistle—drift in the wind
and settle, bombs set to explode when
the ground is disturbed—thief or pioneer—
they seize their opportunities. Each seed
is a finger of life, probing to where life
is not. In extremes of heat, drought and light,
each grows and holds moisture, retards
the wind, casts a spot of shade, and finally
surrenders its substance to others. Each
changes its place a little, reproduces
and perishes and all things follow and
nothing in their basic description prepares
you to witness their ecstasy at living.

Altazor Nursery 3 (Planted 01/92)

Ecstasy of Weeds

Diverse and fertile, weeds wait
Outside a profusion of possibilities.
Lupine lies frozen for ten thousand years;
Thistles rest on fence rows and roadsides;
Chamomile waits to colonize vacant lots.

Our skill at gathering wild plants
And herbs is lost, and with
It the value of weeds—
Who knows that couchgrass heals?

We know nothing of them. Seeking
Leads into wildness: Bluebells,
Rose, spiral racemes.

Where shall my soul dwell?
In immortal tansy.
And where is my home?
On earth in morning glory.

The Ecstasy of Trees

Some things cannot be measured—joy
when light and water stiffen trees
and they stand.
They stand outside
of the plane of ephemeral life,
outside their own dead flesh,
outside the insubstantiality
of light.

Hamadryad Hiding

Hundred-seventy feet high with blue-green needles,
obtuse with small bracts and blue-purple cones—
the tree is so unexpected from the seed.
On my day off: I wanted to try to climb this clean
and dry old pine, set off from the rest.
I jumped up to a low dead limb and pulled myself up,
exultant. I touched and felt
the roughness of the bark, felt the trunk sway
and roots strain with a delicate breeze. I went
up further and looked out across the hills, carefully
not thinking of death or pain or nothingness.

This measured thing is mostly space confounded
by small unpredictabilities, opaque, as impenetrable
to my eyes as to my hands and feet. Emptier now that
the dryads have deserted. I clung securely, moved slowly
higher some hills and valleys shades of brown
and violet-shaded—I saw my body below, shattered
on the needle floor. The branches seemed more treacherous
but I reached the height of a near-by tree, saw
distant mountains and plains. The branches are younger
and firmer but much closer together. I squirmed
through the highest ones, freshened by the wind,
but worried by it all the same. I reached to top—now
I have her height, but she has my mind.
Just to my left, a blasted snag, relict of a moment
when fingers of wood and fingers of lightning met,
and white fire exchanged its life for the life of a pine
leaving mute wood and a black spine.
Swaying, feel the rhythm of respiration lift branches
spread to collect light and cool air around the trunk,
push downwards into the earth to hold and reach out
for minerals and waters—a double life of light and dark,
inside out, a cone of slow fire drawing air, water,
the fire of life drawing earth upwards.

I watched clouds and hawks, as I slowed my breathing
to match her pace. So slow, so long . . .
Later, I tore off a small branch, hurried down,
rubbing bark and skin, heart struggling
with having gotten too close to something unknown,
jumped the last ten feet to the ground, groaning, sighing,
smiling, prize in hand, wearing a crown of needles and lichen,
wondering what kind of change—
She is not solid—there is so much room for spirits
to pass through, unhurried, or perhaps stay. Again
I looked back at transplanted hearts passing
through trees leaving molecular shadows in amber;
the hamadryad has not left, and I am hers.

*(The Greek dryads were conceived by earth [Gaea] from the blood of heaven
[Uranus], who was castrated by his son, Time [Chronos], for refusing to let
his bothers Briareus and Cottus into the light. These nymphs, beautiful females
of divine origin, were given the guardianship of the woods and the trees.
The Wood-nymphs were Dryads, tree-nymphs were Hamadryads, Fruit-
tree nymphs were Meliades, and other nymphs haunted mountains, valleys,
and meadows. The Dryads, who lived in groves were free to move about, in
trees and out. They often associated with Artemis, goddess of the hunt. The
Hamadryads, who dwelled in individual trees, died with their trees— each
tree cried in anguish when cut).*

Cutting a dead limb on a Ponderosa pine

Amphibian Dreams

The arc has been described,
The victim seized.
The tongue recoils, ingesting fly.
The waters smooth and the shiny
Body settles again.
Silence returns to the pond.

His sight a Pythagorean quest
For the meaning of curves;
The eyes transparent, his body
Sinks in the cool murk,
Lord of two mediums.
In formless water, he dreams
Of the sharpness of air.

Upsidedown woodpecker drunk on fermented berries

In an Irish Forest

At a magic convention in Ireland, I scoff at a woman
trying to teleport two people to different places along a wall—
it would be a neat trick if— I scoff again louder.
She invites me to be one. So, I agree. She says, you must say
the words, 'Far Invaray,' three times. I ask three?
She says a mathematician could. I say I am only
an accountant to keep numbers straight.
She says, 'Listen to me count to ten, subtract the two
and count again. Get to six and then eight but be complete
in the witches table nine is one and ten is none.'
Then I count too, and I hold a leg iron on a pipe—
the pipe tingles, but no one moves. I wonder
though about the feeling. She blames me for being skeptical.
We argue throughout the meeting, that first day.
Black eyes. Her name is Cairrean.
That night I buy several ice creams for dinner at a newsstand.
On way to the camp ground, I meet Emer, Tuathla and others.
We talk. My ice cream melts. I sleep on a mound in the park,
near gypsies, cold on damp grass, by an apple tree,
no blankets, no peace from memory. The sharp tongued
winds of the north they thirst for your damp breath.

The next day more weak magic. Cairrean asks me
if I can do magic. I say yes, of sorts. She says: For example?
She and cohort of young nice-looking witches, all slim
with black hair, but different heights, have been teasing me.
I am attracted to Moira, but their teasing is mean
and I do not answer, only listen and observe.
That afternoon, we are all walking in the holly woods
outside Blarney Castle. After a while Cairrean speaks:
'Salamander coil and glow, sylph smile and disappear
Whoever is ignorant of the properties and powers
of the four elements can never master them.'
Nothing happens. I look around and find some willow
poles on the ground, cut a while ago. I find a few nails,
some blocks and make a small set of stilts.
One of the boys, Conchobhar, tries it. I say that is magic!
I make a taller pair, which is used by another girl,

then figure I can make a really tall pair that can only
be reached by someone already on stilts. That works too,
although it is hard to stop and get off. The witches
seem peeved. They ask for real magic. Now.

Then a young deer walks out of the oaks onto the trail
near me. I stay still. The deer walks by me, stops
and touches my hand with her nose. I look at the witches,
then down at the deer's front hooves— blue and green
paisley swirls, almost as if painted. I point out the hooves
to the witches. The deer looks at them, leaps the fence
and bounds back into the trees. Flash of white.
We walk on. The witches ask me if I can call animals.
I say no, only thunder. They ask me if I will. I say no.
But I lower myself down. I crawl like a snake to see
the roots, looking at ants and filaments of fungus—
I stand suddenly. Cairrean says the lightning is near,
the sound of a jay the whir of a bat the newts
are in the bracken the tree roots move like serpents
in the soil. And everything coils and soon we will fill the air.

I cannot answer. But I hold my arms out from my side.
A snowy owl lands on the wire fence opposite me
and sits with both wings outspread. I look; she looks;
everyone looks. She drops off the fence on the other
side to the ground. I think she may fly away.
I put one arm to my side and the other hand on my shoulder.
The owl flies to my shoulder. I move my hand to cover
my head so she won't strike it. She taps
my fingernails with her beak.
I crouch down. The owl drops to the ground. I stroke
her head and back. The younger girls and boys
come closer. I ask them if they would like to touch
the owl. They say yes, and several do tentatively.
I notice the owls claws are painted yellow and red.
The owl flies back to my shoulder; she seems heavier
and larger. I ask her if she is a gypsy. She says,
who? I say I cannot begin to guess her name nor
would I dare assign her one. She says then I cannot
know her. She now has spangles; her legs are longer—

she more resembles a little girl dressed as an owl.
She has colorful cloth with silver threads around
her waist. We talk about magic, its weakness,
disappearance, pretense, and hiding places.

Suddenly it is dawn. She is standing beside me about
four feet tall now. I ask her if she must go. She says
it would be best. I help her to my shoulders to fly
into the woods. She leaps and glides but lands face
down in the grass—she is more girl than owl. I run
to her side and help her up. She blows air over
her feathers in exasperation. Too long, she says. I kiss
her, but her lips are already hard. She is smaller.

I lift her and launch her again into the hazel trees.
As she glides away from me she seems smaller yet.
She lands on a low birch limb, glances back, her neck
twisting all the way around. She flies up to a larger
branch, perhaps confused by the light or just
uncomfortable. Then she glides by an alder tree
in the dark forest, becoming smaller until she is gone.

I look for feathers; there are none. I look at the sky;
it is overcast. Everyone has gone. Not one even
noticed my reconstructed beech forest—
        vanished four thousand years ago.

Beech forest by Vidima

Three Perspectives—September

I.

In the Cork countryside, I walked beside the woods,
looking into the shadows for a source of movement.
I saw none, so I went in. I waited by an oak, alone,
and I waited longer until the shadows covered me.

II.

Someone courted us by walking around and pausing
and coming inside, but he went no further and we could
not move to him. We waited beside him and he waited
beside us, until the ground and shadows connected us.

III.

I saw him walking, then go into the cove and as he
reached into the trees, his arms lengthened
and the roots came up and branches lowered until
I could not tell where tree began and he disappeared.

Three Perspectives—February

I.

I saw her lying beneath an alder, in brown lace;
I went to her and lay down and touched her face.
Her brown hair hung over me and through its veil
I met her eyes and on my side I felt her fingernails.

II.

He appeared, as I was lying with a beam of sun,
his handsome skin, like my fur, shining with health
and need. He lay beside me and offered his life
which I took in my need and made a part of mine.

III.

I watched a man walk directly through the forest
to where a bear lay in the ambient light by her den.
He lay directly down and touched her muzzle; saliva
rolled from her mouth, running down his cheek
as she tore him open with her claws and feasted.

Three Perspectives—November

I.

I was sitting under the alder, admiring the many
mushrooms—my hands reached into the soil
and brought up masses of threads—fungus roots,
the symbiotic net that holds the forest together,
orange, white, gold—I tasted a few. Tired, I lay
down on the spongy forest bed. When I awoke
I felt refreshed, more alert and complete.

II.

She was here, we touched, then my filaments
blended with her flesh, probed her cortex cells,
and what she was missing and what I was missing
balanced. I enhanced her ability to draw elements
from the soil, air and water and she gave me new
elements, a wonderful new mobility, and a way
to speak to the moving others—the eaters.

III.

The forester was sitting under the tree examining
something. She rubbed it, sniffed it, tasted it, smiled
and lay down—colored threads swelled over her
suddenly then receded back into the earth. I paused,
confused by what I had seen. Then she arose, turned
like someone blind, until her eyes focused on me,
golden orange highlights flashed in her irises.

(*The roots of many trees create a symbiotic relationship with an
orange-colored sponge-like fungus called mycorrhiza. The tree
roots provide sustenance to the fungus, which absorbs nitrogen
and minerals that the tree uses. The fungal hyphae decompose
organic matter and cycle the nutrients directly to the host root,
allowing trees to chemically share nutrients and information.*)

Three Perspectives—April

I sat on a rock, cool to the touch, not welcoming.
I saw all the past change from that perspective,
what it was like to grow by accretion that cannot
be measured with heartbeats, what it was like
to be broken by ice and lichens. My bones.

A moment of consciousness but a thousand years
have passed, and the sum of all my consciousness
is the image of forests moving like shadows across
land—and this idea, that moving from a molten
past floating dream to a solid form gives me voice.

She was just a hiker who lay on a rock in the sun
stretched her arms and molded her back to
the curve. She was so still I took her for dead
and grey as the rock underneath. Then the fingers
spread, and a deep thrumming began—

Three Perspectives from an Irish Forest—June

I lay down in a grassy depression. The lines
I thought were roots were bones, as white
as eyes, joined by a thought that the spirit might
match with mine, might offer a wild
pulse to my heart and link to another mind.

The bones rose up and held him lightly, as if
they were mere fingers of light. The form spoke
of its life as a wolf of the wood, how it lived and died,
how it lay down one last time on the pine needles
and let the last breath depart. I heard the sigh.

My spirit found a home, another hunter
as clever and loyal, another expression
of the impulse to breathe, to prowl,
to taste of life, the chance to howl
for every storm, and run and dance.

Haiku Interlude

No position complete,
the goals of sleep, each the same:
to catch and hold you.

Errors and dreams are
the sources of creation
and my life fuels them.

Without the scrawking
jays or rooting trees your sacred
touch is not enough.

My arms are empty
my head full with memory
and that is enough.

Daphne from laurel
your body bends towards me
reversing the chase.

Peel an onion
by layers—at the center
of unity—nothing.

On a trail through woods
a spider clings to my arm—
stickiness of life.

Somewhere grey mountains
lift a purple sky watched
 just by me, serenely

There are things about
light we cannot measure—
joy when light stiffens trees.

Wolf is flesh, deer is
flesh, grass is flesh—all flesh light
many facets gone.

Waiting on meters
the wrens are patient for bugs
smashed on car bumpers.

Sitting on the tip
of the pine, the cardinal
hinges it to sky.

Playing on the bole
of an oak, squirrel spirals
downward—shadow tail.

Thorned thistle, tender,
pushes its way through concrete—
always rock-breaker.

Struck by hot lightning
the oak raises its bare limbs
in astonishment.

False Senryu Word Nests

Lying in bed ear
to ear, rib to rib, again
accosting me you

Struggling to speak to
be heard to gain prizes of
public agony

Land is built, ocean
done and I have only just
arrived to shore.

The highest tree is
astonished by the storm and
burns in the dark rain.

Bear is the eyebrow
on the forest's face, raised to
express its surprise.

The brown skeleton
calmly yields its branches and
boughs to the bonfire.

The lynx and the green
tree take the secret helix
to a calm twilight

Amaryllis, crane,
and bear charm their mates until
they are free as clouds.

Only idiots
cannot imagine copies
of prime ideas (—being private and original).

The cloud's complexion
of ideas turns them in-
to forms of windows.

Prose traces the straight
furrow, but verse turns it in-
side out, insults it.

Snag at Mountain Grove Forest

Paion   (wherein the author calendars a charm
for complexing comrades while cranes
climb clouds with pedigrees)

Land is laid
The ocean is done
and I have only just arrived.

The first step is ambiguous
the second becomes ambition
and the third destination

Vestiges trace the verse.
Alternate footprints pave the halo
in miniature on colonized ground.
Weeds and their ideas grow
larger without lines.

The seeds are spread in wisps
that blind the window
and profit weeds.

The secret is not in the helix
nor in the flesh
but the living curved expression.

We fashioned a pyramid
with ourselves at the top
but we are only hybrids of ideas.

Angels without enthusiasm
are like bees without
melilotus
            not free
but lost barren imaginings.

The brown heart
of the bear consents to a bonfire
of boughs and branches.

Astonished by green flame
the lynx is calm and watchful
in the twilight.

Raven is noisy, no
raven is noise
airsick and uncertain.

Infant insults a mouse
Idiot sharks an idea
Squirrel monsters disorder—None speak.

Struggling to speak
to be heard amidst the
agony of many, we open.

Wine has its other uses
in the symposium of life
than to fill skeletons.

Lying in grass imbricating,
accosting each other, learning
stillness and silence.

An apple tree in Altazor orchard

Facets of Light (Marishimia Letter Play)

Riashamimi Reflected

I saw your face in the window
of a 1956 ford, looking forlornly
at the signs that passed
and I ached to comfort you and tell
you that your sadness would pass
but I waited and you were gone
with the flow of Boston traffic.

Years later, on the sidewalk
in New York we passed and I saw
that you were resigned to
whatever fate you thought held you
and I wanted to tell you that
we could make a better ending,
but I paused again, too long.

Later, many decades later,
on Coeur d'Alene as my boat was speeding
by the shore I saw you sitting
on the dock looking at the water
send its messages in waves
and I ached to hold you until
you looked at me that way.

And over all these years I waited wanted
and ached for someone I never knew
and so was unable to know those already
near me and I may die pining for what
can never be but I ache to see you
one more time and stop you and say,
at last, please stay with me.

Amishimira in Blue

That day that you wore the blue
print dress, I took the time
to look deeply into your eyes—
from the dress to your eyes
I moved to an infinity of blue—

                              no

I would be foolish to compare
your eyes to a shallow lake
or to the thin extent of sky.
I know better: In the constellation
of Orion, there are stars that color
of blue, and only magnitudes
of distance shield us from
their furnaces of creation—
and only distance from you now
saves me from total
annihilation.

Miriamisha Through Tearlight

I was happy with you in dreams
but I was afraid to speak them
to you, realizing our love had never
been and could never be—I kept
my feelings from you, and wept
for the loss of possibility.

But, each tear, painfully torn
and exquisitely formed,
then seen through, revealed
other dreams with you,
other lives, and now my reason
for weeping is to visit those
worlds inside—

In each world a new life unfolds
and in each I find you waiting
and in each I weep and subdivide
until my lives infinitely recede
like rows of self-reflecting mirrors,
yet I believe that what the tears
separate, eventually will unite.

Amimishari in Dreams

That night after we talked
in the quiet center of
a crowded Dupnitsa sidewalk
I dreamed that we became lovers,
seamlessly and completely,
then after a while
married, lived together,
had a daughter, Geveya,
worked side by side
and aged under our tree,
then I died, and you both
mourned me quietly.

But, now, after work, when
I meet you on the sidewalk,
I have to smile, because I see
you have our daughter's eyes.

Shamirimia On Silk

In this decadent dream you invited
me with your eyes (shaded by those
incredible lashes) to lay down beside
you on white silk pillows—that
moment is forever fixed in memory:
Your hair fanned out in a halo
of dark curls, your skin made darker
by contrast with the sheet,
the shine of moisture on your lips,
the darker hair of your belle chose,
small bruise on delicately curled toes,
the threads of small details tied
us to that extended moment
while I waited, before descending
to eclipse your glowing face—

Mariamishi in Wild Flight

The music was wild and never-ending—
your feet hardly touched the ground
before resuming their flight
turning you around
without stopping.
From a distant orbit I tried to match
your pattern, to match your joy
at moving and flow in a flight
of expression, without direction
without reason.
I stopped dancing—you continued.
I watched and in you I saw
beauty without awareness,
laughter without pain.
Then, in myself, I saw love
without desire, love without
words, until
now.

Horses Under Lightning

All afternoon warm humid air rose above
the hill overlooking Potlatch, Idaho.
The horses were pastured in the orchard
in the portable electric corral by the house.

I brushed insect eggs from the black hair
on Roma's chest. You doctored the cut
on Figurina's leg; we both had to push
Ballerina's nose from our work. You said
she has to be trained soon. She nickered
agreement and we laughed. The dark bay
looked just like her mother. Then we talked
on the porch as the sun set to the sounds
of horses grazing. Roma stood guard
against every shadow or unexplained
motion. The air was still unstable, waiting
to be overturned. Unseen in the forming
cloud the collision of moving particles
redistributed charges.

We went to bed as the cloud built over
us and slept until violent booms woke us.
The cloud had reached maturity, smashing
air, rattling the windows with hard rain.
The horses screamed.

With a dead flashlight and an empty lantern
we went outside to calm the horses.
The rain soaked us instantly, one gasp
and it was already too late to go back
inside. The absolute dark forced us to stop
and wait less than three feet from the house.

We had to wait for each flash for a tenth
of a second of light before moving a step
closer, after which the darkness deepened
even more. I took Roma, you the mother
and daughter. I did not want to be there,

but the barn was half a mile away. We had
to keep them from running. Roma
was wild and rearing, each movement became
a still picture illuminated by a stroke of light;
I reached her on the fourth try. I stroked
her neck and withers slowly with one hand
keeping the other on her chest to track her.
I whispered soothingly into her nose—a bolt
showed white starred face and frightened eyes.

It was like being on the floor of the factory
of creation where electric power—ten
thousand amps, a hundred million volts,
per bolt—surged between the generators.
Charges built between the negative cloud
and its positive shadow on the earth until
they exceeded the insulation of air. The current
flowed in a path and the return stroke flared
with the heat of the sun. The path and stroke
hit too fast to tell apart. A crack and instantly
a bang as air exploded. My teeth hurt
my ears hurt. I saw the sound bounce off
every thing—I saw the waves vibrate air
and trunks of trees. I watched as a tall cedar
down the slope—my favorite for sitting under—
was struck—twenty foot shards were rammed
into the ground around the trunk, an instant
perfect wooden cone—a small flame flickered
at the ruined vertex, then went out.

Another strike destroyed the southwest corner
fencepost, you said. I saw you now and then
made still by a flash. I felt myself absorbing
energy somehow or maybe just vibrating
in sympathy. The horses were wild. The night,
the light, was wild. I saw it through them.

After an hour the lightning moved northeast,
rumbling as different parts of the cloud reported
their progress, or differences with the ground,

or unhappiness with the attitude of another,
light flashing between them. The air
had turned and balance was restored.
All things recharged. The rain became
steady. The horses were calm and hung
their heads in the rain. We stood beside
them, looking up. I did not want to move.

We went back inside, left clothing soaked
on the porch. Every night since is pallid
and dull, except sometimes when I look
in your eyes or Roma's and see the ghosts
of lightning.

Wild Strawberries

On the way to fix the fence
I walked over them, but
you called me back—hundreds
of tiny, ripe, wild strawberries,
almost invisible in the grasses.

We lay down in a patch and fed
each other berries, hardly
aware that the horses had
gathered in the corner
looking to see if we would share
them (we did).

I suppose we fixed the fence
eventually and rode the horses
up the road, but of all the good
times that we planned and had
I remember this accidental
moment and smile—I swear
that I can still taste
the juice that graced
our lips.

Tangled Light

Marishimia Dancing

Music filtered through turning leaves
and lights made columns of trees.
He stood and spiraled his hand, fingers
out, and she nodded and rose
in perfect communication
Their paths converged;
They locked arms and began to dance.
An unsteady alliance at first
subject to the rise and fall
of distant music, the hollows
of one body accepted the swells
of the other. The air seemed warmer
the music louder, the colors of their clothing
contrasted and blended as they moved.
Thought created patterns
made by their feet.

They held each other closely, whirled
then pushed apart and played arpeggios
in light. They pulled together
and spun faster, their steps
not limited by the music
as the music changed to fit
the steps. Once they became tangled
and fell, but the music paused for
laughter and it was apropos.
At times the limbs would intertwine
in a hopeless tangle
until one would rise like a snake
charmed from a basket
and the rest would disengage
and flow away.

Then they would break away
from the other dancers
and commence a chase across the floor.

The dance was a flame
between them that flickered
as they moved and blazed
again stronger as they touched.
Light strung lines
wherever they went until
the world was a shining
web and at the center, their dance.

Evening Swifts

When I was younger every word
was weighted
by my own feelings. Now, much later,
I ask how
do these words make you feel? Warm?
Worried? Sad?
Did they open a door, or close one?
Did they release
you to flight? Or wind you tighter
in a circle?
Or do they mean nothing?
You do not need to answer.
The evening I dreamed
that you were looking up at my window
from the street
I was watching swifts feed on unseen
prey rolling and swerving
then visiting
nests under the eaves of human houses.
Not being
weighed down by words they flew
so perfectly.

Gathering Layers

When we kissed the first time, it was with the shock
of never having kissed before—oh, no
it was with the freshness of rain that, having fallen,
evaporated then precipitated to renew
itself, and that was the kiss.

When we touched the first time, it was the unexpected
Otherness of a mirror image—no, no
it was like the surfacing of a stone buried for geological
time, exposed again by movements
so sublime . . .

Every kiss, every touch, should be so and yet gather layers
that reveal the original each time,
like a geode. You have no past—no, you do,
but it is what shaped you and what, with mine, brought
us together—

Let memory be stripped by evaporation, the burden
of experience be lifted by the lightness of—no,
rather let the whole knotted fabric
of life simply unfold,
and us within.

Threads

In the new threads of the avocado
seed lining the vase,
I see everything that is gentle
in you made visible.
In the marble plate under the vase,
I see everything that is strong
in you made visible.

My life is so tied
to you that everything is shaped
by connection and strength—

the marble resists water and weight;
the threads could crack marble;
the weight of time disperse threads.

The voice that tries
to speak is carried long afterwards
in threads and marble
as faint echoes in matter
and as memory in written words.

Changing Lightly

Things fall away
from us like leaves useless
to trees in winter. We keep what
we need, and rather than use
dead memories for defense,
we let them decay to prepare
the soil for regeneration.

You worried that your past
is an unwanted burden on the delicate
threads that connect us,
but, experience should not weigh
us down like unwanted baggage;
it should contribute
to our transparency
so that our thoughts, our motives,
are perfectly clear, and eventually
we will not be seen at all
standing in front of the mountains.

Leaf

You always present yourself like a leaf
that can be turned
and examined, nothing hidden, but I
want to photograph your mystery by
brushing your hair across your eyes
like Veronica Lake. Then I look again
and realize that what is hidden
can never be seen or understood, even
through actions like turning.

So, I think of you now as unknowable—
Every movement a mysterious expression
of some secret invisible being
using ordinary motions
to create simple patterns
that no one can decipher.

Perhaps if one pattern
contained a kiss
I would be still.
Or not.

The living room at Altazor Palace

Masks

The Moon as a Mask for the Earth

The sun
       and earth double-bodied
Behind the moon
     dance and twirl
around in space
      and from Neptune
a point of light behind
       a pock-marked face.

Dust as the Mask of Chaos

He drops the small chalk
      to the floor   brushes his hands
    stands
scratching more signs
      on the blackboard's surface
          connections
to invisible sorcery
             The secret rests
in the chaos of dust on the floor.
          Incandescent light
    leaves the window.

Metal as the Mask of Energy

     Ghosts in metal
   of particles from the center,
the iridescent center of the earth
      murmurings distilled
   from hard collisions; radiation
from its primordial being trapped
      in matter patterns
    from cycles of stars and faintly

glowing bodies. Stars
　　　have history and it lives
in human memory. Faint pulses
　　　　　from the sun echo
　　　in waves in the brain.
The rhythm of the sea invades
　　　　　the copper-lead of dreams.
　　　The battery made and charged
remembers ghosts in metal.

The Visible as Mask for the Invisible

The unnoticed are invisible, the very small
the very large, the patterns of the infinitely
complex and unfinished
time.
　　　The visible exposes the hidden
if the mask is good, if it intertwines the invisible
with its easy strands
　　　　　　　　　enabling the weak
to see the strong
　　　　　　　threads, enabling people
to become the unseen animals and gods

The face was made of leaves and shadows
mouth opening
　　　　　　　to a dark maw. The eyes complex veins
　　　of leaves
　　　　　　　one leaf, then another, frees its stem
　　　and weaves a spiraled loop—
The leaf we see in turning
becomes invisible and another appears. This
　　is the operation of mystery: Leaves turn
and present us with the strangeness
of a hidden side. They tease us
　　　　　　　from a different
perspective, the leaf we think
we know turns and disappears; the new
side visible

We see and name it
                              and
it becomes invisible again. Leaves acquire full
existence by turning.
              Turning is revelation: secrets
Open. Things turn
                    and are renewed.
                                        Which way
              do wolves turn, before lying down?
Which way do whirlpools turn
                                Or whirlwinds?
The twist of oak or sycamore; the maze
of tree roots, branches, lichen, rock and moss;
The twist of a hole
                    dug by a skunk;
snakes coiling; the lay of balsam fronds;
Hawks wheeling,
                    shrikes hunting;
the turn of a shell; the helix of light or
      the spin of galaxies?'

Sound as a Mask for the Visible

The parts lack visible
                          connection, but a minnow
recognizes another minnow,
        and birds hear other
birds as each marks out
a territory. Birds inform the fish
of the Pacific about the state
of vegetation
in the Cascades. Each living being
has its own sphere and these all overlap
around the earth until the whole hissing
      yipping network deafens space;
the bark of a fox or twitter
of a sparrow contribute
to the whole. The earth is a great
                    round noisy beast.

Light as the Mask of Darkness

Elements fuse
      in the hearts of stars
light is the waste.
        After millions of years
in the center
    light is pushed
toward the cup of space
      binding emptiness together
tracing the geometry of chaos.
      The world is made with light
reweaving its mesh
        countless times with reflections
from the ground, moon and sea
    before it leaves.

Shadow as the Mask of Light

Shadow is not absence
   but the signature of motion
it is the way—all motion turns to heat.
   You burn and rise
from the ashes like a phoenix
    burned the wind stirs
the ashes and you rise—
      sky darkening with streaming lines of rain
helix turning and the code remaining
     ashes expanding and steaming
something moves and tears its way out.
      Dark nebula
Molten red element bird renewed
   Your feathers are now metallic
You alter yourself to survive
   But only you notice the change
And the change is irreversible.
   How much of your life
does the shadow take as its own?

Flesh as Mask for Shadow

Leaves grow at angles from the stem
so each can collects the light.
                              light falls slowly
like the dust that leaves collect
                              it is held
and its crust forms the mask
                              we see
The leaves are burned by day
                              thin dry pages
that once transmuted the sun to flesh
lie folded like stale meanings.

Consciousness as the Mask of Flesh

Face in sandstone   thirty-degrees
        a fireplace, bicycle parts, a fly wing
            The expression on the face
Debussy as he was composing   passionate flesh.
            We reduce expressions to words
and these are covered over by the motions
of living.
            Feelings fade and form a sediment
Pressure from the weight of feelings compresses
Memories into layers, and these are heated
like carbon in rock and assume
        a crystalline form.
Continents of consciousness float
on layers of dense experience. The self-world
is composed of thousands of feet
of ragged memories.
            Plates broken by shifting,
                float on a molten
        core   heaved by inner turmoil
Pieces penetrate the surface
            and invite a deeper archaeology. The mind
excavates them and elevates them to the air
                again and to clouds.

Sleep as the Mask of Consciousness

She lay on her side, indifferent
      in sleep. Slowly music, and light
Dancers around a fire
      One held up a metal disk
—She woke, gazing at the wall—
its smoothness dissolved as from acid
on a copper Sesterce—Vespacian's profile
She blinked redimensioning
The smoothness was scored with scratches
      As she watched Scratches outlined figures
Sharply across a fissure
the code of mystery renewed in red.

Dream as the Mask of Sleep

We live in a metaphysics of light
and only need to look to this cathedral
to be reminded. We have created a glass
forest of filtered mists where radiance is stained
and dimmed to fit our minds. And the dream
restores the connections of the invisible
threads. And waking is forgotten.
And when the sun sets behind
the sea, its last ray is green.

Author Biography   A. M. Caratheodory was born at the time of the largest solar eruption ever recorded—a fact he discovered when he became interested in astronomy. After basic schooling in Virginia, he attended the University at Charlottesville, where he studied astrophysics. His work on mathematical models of stars received awards from NSF, NASA, USN, USAF, Bausch & Lomb, and others.

Dropping out of school as a conscientious objector and peace activist, he was drafted. He enlisted in the Air Force, working as a microwave researcher, satellite track technician, medical corpsman, and janitor. After an honorary discharge, he worked as an observer, then research associate in astrophysics for a number of installations, including the MIT Cambridge Research Labs, Lunar and Planetary Lab, and the University of Arizona's Steward Observatory.

Returning to school, he took courses in psychology, biology, and ecology. On various research grants, he studied wolves throughout the northern hemisphere, forests on the northwest coast of North America, and lakes in Sothwest Florida. Since then, he started his own business in ecological design.

Finding that his experience followed Auden's prescription for poets, he has written in poetic, as well as scientific, forms. He has been published in numerous regional journals; since 1984, he has worked only on book-length themes. He continues to work hard to keep to the dictates of Wordsworth and Novalis to be a good poet.

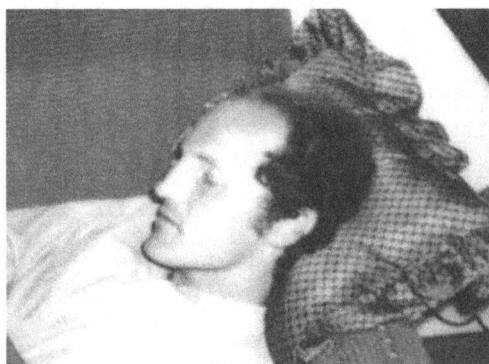

Colophon

Design: Deer Designs (Africa, America & Asia Deer)
Graphics: A, M. Caratheodory
Photographs: C.A.M. Woulfe
Author Photograph: Meredith Nieman
Display text: Gillsans Light
Body text: Baskerville
Formatting: Indesign on a Mac G5

The kitchen at Altazor Palace

Altazor Orchard in May

Printed in the USA